All the King's men.

Angels Fall

Angels Fall

A PLAY BY

Lanford Wilson

A MERMAID DRAMABOOK

Hill and Wang · New York

A division of Farrar, Straus and Giroux

Published simultaneously in Canada
by McGraw-Hill Ryerson Ltd., Toronto

Printed in the United States of America

FIRST HILL AND WANG EDITION, 1983

Library of Congress Cataloging in Publication Data
Wilson, Lanford.
Angels fall.
(A Mermaid dramabook)
I. Title.
PS3573.I458A83   1983   812'.54   83–97
ISBN 0–8090–2648–1
ISBN 0–8090–1245–6 (pbk.)

For
Lou Fink

Angels Fall was commissioned and first presented by The New World Festival, Inc., in Miami, Florida, on June 19, 1982.

Director / Marshall W. Mason
Setting / John Lee Beatty
Costumes / Jennifer Von Mayrhauser
Lighting / Dennis Parichy
Sound / Chuck London Media / Stewart Werner
Production Stage Manager / Fred Reinglas

The cast, in order of appearance, was as follows:

Niles Harris / Fritz Weaver
Vita Harris / Nancy Snyder
Don Tabaha / Danton Stone
Marion Clay / Tanya Berezin
Salvatore (Zappy) Zappala / Brian Tarantina
Father William Doherty / Richard Seff

Barnard Hughes (for whom the role was written) replaced Mr. Seff as Father Doherty when the play opened at the Circle Repertory Company in New York City on October 16, 1982. Original music for this production was by Norman L. Berman.

This production was moved intact to the Longacre Theatre on January 18, 1983. It was produced by Elliot Martin, Circle Repertory, Lucille Lortel, The Shubert Organization, and The Kennedy Center.

The shepherd's brow, fronting forked lightning, owns
The horror and the havoc and the glory
Of it. Angels fall, they are towers, from heaven—a story
Of just, majestical, and giant groans.
But man—we, scaffold of score brittle bones;
Who breathe, from groundlong babyhood to hoary
Age gasp; whose breath is our memento mori—
What bass is our *viol for tragic tones?*

GERARD MANLEY HOPKINS

Angels Fall

CHARACTERS

NILES HARRIS, fifty-six, an art historian and professor. He is tall, elegant, and disheveled.

VITA HARRIS, thirty, his wife, thin and strikingly attractive.

SALVATORE (ZAPPY) ZAPPALA, twenty-one, almost skinny, quite energetic, a professional tennis player.

MARION CLAY, early forties, a gallery owner, handsome, well turned out.

DON TABAHA, mid-twenties, half-Indian, intense.

FATHER WILLIAM DOHERTY, sixty-five, the parish priest.

PLACE

A small and very plain adobe mission in northwestern New Mexico.

We see the entrance, where a bell hangs just outside the front door, and the entire interior of the church. Wooden benches without backs, a simple altar painted with faded blue and yellow; the only decoration is a washed wainscoting and a primitive painting of the Madonna, painted on a round barrel top. The front door leads to a sandy parking lot where (offstage) there is a telephone. Across the room from the front door is another door leading to an equally sandy garden that might, space permitting, include a few wooden crosses over bare graves. On one side of the altar is a door to the living quarters.

It is five in the afternoon, Saturday, early June.

Act One

The interior of the church is dark and cool. White-hot sunlight streaks in from the narrow, deep-set windows. Outside, the light is intense. DON TABAHA *sits alone, staring at the wall. After a moment he rises and goes into the residence. We hear people approaching the front door from the parking lot.*

NILES: (*Offstage*) We'll look at the map and see if we can find some semblance of a decent highway.

VITA: (*Offstage*) It's enough just to get out of this glare.

NILES: (*Offstage*) It must be two hours to the nearest motel.

VITA: (*Appears at the doors. They open. Sunlight illuminates the interior of the church*) Hey, it's open. We're in luck.

NILES: (*Standing in the open doorway*) Thank God.

VITA: (*Her voice lowered*) It's wonderfully cool; that sun is blazing. (*For the first time they look around them*) You sit, and I'll go see if that telephone works.

NILES: I don't want to sit. I want to get back on the road. (*He sits*)

VITA: I'll be a sec. (*She goes off. Niles moves to the window, looks out after her. He takes a prescription bottle from his pocket, has difficulty opening it, peers into the bottle, dumps the only pill onto his hand*)

NILES: Sanctuary. (*He looks into the empty bottle, carefully breaks the pill in half, and returns half to the bottle*) Well, half a sanctuary. (*He looks around the church. There is water in the font; he decides against that and moves to the garden doors. As they open, the interior grows lighter. Niles sees what he is looking for and goes out the door. The church is empty for a moment*)

VITA: (*Entering*) Niles? Are you all right?

NILES: (*Offstage*) Just a minute.

VITA: (*Notices the pill bottle, picks it up, smiling at the half pill. Calling*) Where have you got to? (*Puts the bottle in her purse*)

NILES: (*Offstage*) I found a water faucet I'm sure hasn't been opened in twenty years. I'll die of typhoid, but I'll die refreshed. (*He re-enters, wiping his face with a damp handkerchief*) I must have half of New Mexico on my face.

VITA: You were beginning to look a little like a cinnamon doughnut, yes.

NILES: Sixty miles on a dirt road with nothing to look at except sagebrush, only to be turned back by the highway patrol and have to look at the same sagebrush all over again from the other side. You told Dr. Singer we'll be a day late?

VITA: He's in a meeting. His secretary has gone to the bank.

NILES: At twelve hundred dollars a day per shrunken head, you'd think Singer's institute would own the bank by now.

VITA: I left the number of the pay phone out there.

NILES: Darling, I'm not going to stand in a church in the middle of the wilderness waiting for some secretary to return our call.

VITA: If we don't hear in ten minutes, I'll try again. (*NILES notices the pill bottle is gone*) I've got it.

NILES: Good. I may need it. (*Looks at his watch*) We'll give her five minutes. (*He spreads a handkerchief on the deep sill of the window, and sits*) Even when we get there, Phoenix is going to be no fun for you. Living down the road from the asylum—in some sleazy motel.

VITA: Holiday Inn. No surprises.

NILES: Probably be crowded with husbands and wives of the other patients, all brightly pretending nothing is wrong. Keeping active and interested and fit. Forming a slow-pitch softball team. I see T-shirts emblazoned with WIVES OF THE LOONIES. (*He gets up again*)

VITA: I'll skip that, I think. I might even get some work done.

NILES: I'm sure after one session of whatever it is they do to me, I'll be infinitely grateful for your presence close at hand. (*Looking around*) Good Lord, this church is unrelentingly severe. No self-respecting Catholic should tolerate this degree of austerity.

VITA: I imagine the locals would rip off anything not nailed down. There's a sign over the pay phone that says: "This phone is for medical emergencies only. If you need money, break the Coke machine."

NILES: Oh, dear.

VITA: I checked. Sure enough, the Coke machine is broken.

NILES: (*Looking out*) Can we even hear the telephone from this distance? Hello. One of those desert surprises. There's a wonderful broad luteous patch of something. I don't have my glasses. A really marvelous yellow hazing over by the road. Some thriving cactus or other.

VITA: That's a bulldozer.

NILES: Really.

VITA: It looks like they're widening the road.

NILES: Of course they're widening the road. We didn't pass a single car coming or going, what better place to widen the road?

(DON *says something in Navaho offstage. He enters from residence.* VITA *jumps.* DON *wears a University of New Mexico T-shirt*)

VITA: Oh!

DON: How'd you get in here?

NILES: I beg your pardon?

DON: The church is closed on Saturdays. This isn't a tourist attraction here.

NILES: Yes, we gathered as much.

VITA: We just stopped to use the phone.

DON: That phone is for medical emergencies only.

VITA: Yes, I saw the sign. My husband is checking into a clinic tomorrow. We're going to be delayed. I wanted to let them know nothing serious is wrong.

DON: Then there's no emergency.

VITA: We seem to be encroaching on alien territory.

NILES: Are you the vicar around here?

DON: The more devout of my tribe come in to pray for the maize.

NILES: In the event the summer corn dance doesn't suffice.

VITA: Are you at the University of New Mexico? (*Beat*) They had another really great basketball team this year.

DON: Come on, the church is closed.

VITA: I noticed a *portale* out back. We can wait back there if we can hear the phone.

DON: Don't go back there. That's private back there. The Tabahas live in back.

MARION: (*Offstage*) At least get out of the damn heat.

DON: (*Going to the door*) Marion! What the . . . ?

VITA: (*Overlapping*) There's someone else. Where did they come from?

DON: (*Turning to them*) Cameras are against tribal law. Outside of that, like I said, make yourselves at home. (*Exits into parking lot*)

VITA: Oh, my.

NILES: There are people who, when you meet them, bring to mind all the things you might have done but neglected to do. Such as learn to handle firearms.

(*A motorcycle starts up and drives off*)

VITA: Apparently that was his Honda out there. He's kicking up a duststorm.

MARION: (*Offstage*) Don!

VITA: It amazes me how cool you become in the face of those types.

NILES: Altogether too much experience. Much too much experience.

MARION: (*Offstage*) Ridiculous! Is this the pits? If we can't get the airport, I'll try the damn base or the—I don't know—weather. Of all the stupid. (*Enters counting change. ZAP hangs back in the doorway*) I'm blind from that damn sun. Twenty, thirty, forty—give me your dimes.

ZAP: (*Sees NILES and VITA*) Hi.

VITA: Hi.

NILES: How do you do.

MARION: Oh, hi. Sorry. Pisser of a situation, isn't it?

VITA: Very inconvenient for anyone with a tight schedule, yes.

ZAP: We're trying to make a plane.

VITA: Oh, no.

MARION: (*Leaving*) I should be used to it by now. (*To* ZAP) Stay. Stay where it's cool. (*She exits to lot*)

ZAP: No, I'm okay. Good to meet you. (*Exits*)

VITA: Good luck.

MARION: (*Offstage*) I forgot my purse. Go get my purse.

(ZAP *comes back for Marion's purse; exits*)

VITA: What do you suppose is the nature of that relationship?

NILES: *Le coeur a ses raisons que la raison ne connait point.*

VITA: I'm hip.

NILES: (*Looks out front door*) There goes the phone for the next however long. Ah, well. I wish you talked me out of buying these shoes. They're wonderfully comfortable, but they're very stupid-looking.

VITA: I think they're cute.

NILES: Ummm. Cute. I'm afraid I agree with you. I wonder if I dare smoke.

DOHERTY: (*Entering from the garden, talking to himself*) "And the road was a ribbon of moonlight, over the purple moor." (*Sees* NILES *and* VITA) Oh, dear goodness.

NILES: Perhaps not.

DOHERTY: I have no concept of time. I'm sure I've kept you waiting. (*Calls*) Maria! (*Back to them*) Well, she won't come out as long as you're here. Well, then, just to leap right in with both feet, we call these little talks pre-Cana conferences. Water into wine, remember. *Accipite armaturam dei.*

VITA: No, Father, we're not here for religious instruction.

DOHERTY: You're not here for the conference. In spite of everything you've undoubtedly heard of me, I do that rather well. Then you're— Don't help me, it'll come to me.

VITA: No, we're just— No, you see, we— No, we're just stopping—

DOHERTY: No, no, no, no, now. (*Beat*) You know, I'm not even going to try. This is terrible. I'm an absolute blank. You'll have to fill me in.

NILES: Oh, dear.

VITA: We have no appointment. We're just taking advantage of the open door to wait for a telephone call. We just ducked into the church to get out of the sun.

DOHERTY: Oh, I'm very glad, because right at the moment I have kinda a full plate.

VITA: (*Looking out*) Well good, she's giving up. I can try again.

NILES: (*Grabbing at her*) Darling.

VITA: There are so many green valleys and such beautiful mountains. And we expected New Mexico to be a burning desert from end to end.

DOHERTY: That's south of here. You're lost, then; no one finds the place unless they're lost.

VITA: No, we were turned back at the fork, so to speak. There's a bridge out.

DOHERTY: There's no bridge out. Where would there be a bridge out?

NILES: Route 57, about twenty miles north of here.

DOHERTY: No, no, no, no. There couldn't be a bridge out. There's no bridge. I've never heard of the road being impassable in June. We'll be in for the light rains soon, if they come; the gentle rains, the "she-rains" they call them, isn't that lovely? There's no bridge out. It's some problem with the nuclear thing again. The radio was saying something about it. I never listen, but it's good company when you're driving along. I'm not really so rushed, I'm just like this. I'll learn to relax one day. (*Singsong*) Learn to relax, learn to relax. Now. Maybe I can interest you in the fifty-cent tour.

NILES: Some problem with the nuclear thing again?

DOHERTY: There usually is, and they usually say something coy like the bridge is out. We don't pay much attention anymore. Don didn't come through here, did he? Short, dark, surly . . . ?

VITA: In and out.

DOHERTY: In from where and out to where?

VITA: In from there and out on a Honda in a cloud of dust.

DOHERTY: (*Sitting*) Oh, no. Oh, dear.

VITA: Is there something wrong?

DOHERTY: (*Gets up, goes out the front door. Pleasantly*) Yes, of course, anything you like.

NILES: He's not really rushed, he's just like that.

VITA: You are going to be nice.

NILES: I am not. I have every intention of being inordinately difficult. What nuclear thing?

DOHERTY: (*Entering, crossing to the residence door. Happy; to himself*) Ho-ho-ho, ho-ho-ho. He's down at the intersection having a violent argument with Arthur, our highway patrolman.

NILES: Excuse us, but—

DOHERTY: Ho-ho-ho. Ho-ho-ho. (*Exits*)

NILES: This country would do it to the best of them. On the

other hand, I doubt if they'd send the best of them to this country.

DOHERTY: (*Re-enters with binoculars*) Now we'll see. Ho-ho-ho. (*Leaning into the window, looking off*) Oh, what an argument. Arthur's not going to let him pass. Ho-ho-ho.

NILES: Excuse us, but what problem are they having with what nuclear thing again?

DOHERTY: (*Not turning from the window*) No, no, no alarm. Nothing to be alarmed about. They just have these little . . . emergencies.

NILES: Do you find that at all reassuring?

VITA: Let's go with the idea that the bridge is out.

DOHERTY: We had a wonderful fright three years ago. Radio-active clouds drifting across the street. You couldn't see the store. We all hid inside, waiting to be evacuated, but I guess they thought we weren't worth the trouble. Nobody came, nobody came. The next morning men went through in Jeeps, mind you, dressed for the moon, with little radioactive bleepers that were clicking their heads off. You've never heard such a racket. Like a nest of rattlesnakes. And they said: "No, no, no problem. Nothing to be alarmed about. Minor levels, minor levels." They had to yell it out over the sound of the clickers, you understand. And off they went. I had a good laugh at myself when I realized that I had been concerned about the possibility of being rendered sterile. (*Turns to the window*) Oh, now they're both angry. Our patrolman was a classmate of Don's and he enjoys teasing him. Ho-ho-ho. Well, I had better make myself scarce.

NILES: Excuse me, Father—

DOHERTY: Doherty. Bill Doherty. The Indians can't pronounce it—they call me Father Bill. When none of my superiors is around.

NILES: Niles Harris; my wife, Vita. Not that we're alarmed, but what sort of nuclear thing is having these little emergencies?

DOHERTY: Oh, does it matter? I'm sorry, but you would ask. They're trying to install a dump south of here. We're not going to let them get away with that. And over west are about seven mines and mills, and east of here the Rio Puerco goes awash with some kind of waste every few months, and of course there's the reactor at Los Alamos and the missile base down at White Sands, and all kinds of things are seeping into everyone's water. It's all the Perils of Pauline, but I just get into trouble every time I say anything about it. We aren't supposed to notice. Apparently they own this part of the state. Or everything that isn't owned by Texas.

ZAP: (*Offstage*) I can't leave them in the car. They'll warp in the heat, you know that.

DOHERTY: (*Looks out*) Good gracious, what's Marion doing down here? Of course, settling the estate. Poor dear woman. Such a waste. So sad. Still, there's hope. Well, we get them all.

ZAP: (*Entering*) Jeez. Boy. Hi. Boy oh, boy oh, boy.

DOHERTY: This is the only public phone in the village, I'm afraid.

VITA: So we gathered.

DOHERTY: So this is the hot corner. (*Exits into quarters*)

VITA: No luck?

ZAP: Oh, boy. Who knows? We can't get through; every-body's callin' everybody. The airport's busy, the highway patrol's busy, the weather station's busy. We've been listen-ing on the car radio.

VITA: (*As* MARION *enters*) What did they say?

ZAP: Something went wrong trying to get a plane loaded over at the Chin Rock mine.

NILES: We were turned back on Route 57. They said the bridge was out.

MARION: I love the way they don't even try to make their stories plausible.

VITA: There's no bridge on 57?

MARION: Not one. The radio said there's no cause for alarm, but as a precaution they've stopped traffic for a hundred miles.

NILES: Oh, lovely.

ZAP: Oh, boy; oh, boy; oh, boy . . .

MARION: Stay inside. There's no point in wearing yourself out.

ZAP: I know, I know.

MARION: We're due in San Diego. He has a tennis match tomorrow in the opening round of the WCT.

VITA: Oh, no.

ZAP: And this is just great psychological preparation. This is just the perfect psychological preparation.

MARION: I know.

ZAP: Assuming we even get there at all, this is just the best preparation I can think of. Boy, boy, boy, boy, boy. (*He exits*)

MARION: We'll get there. (*Calling*) Don't walk around in the sun. Well, don't fall down. Get the thermos and come and take your zinc. Okay? (*Turning back*) Oh, Lord. Total child.

NILES: (*Rather private*) Ah, well . . . what route did you decide on?

VITA: (*Consulting the road map*) How do you feel about . . . There's Taos. We could visit their little art colony. That might be fun.

NILES: Under no circumstances.

VITA: They would love you. After your review of that dreadful book . . . ?

NILES: *Contemporary Paintings of the American West.*

VITA: Some of the things you said about—what did you call it?

NILES: Regional Art. Exactly. We'd both be stoned at the gate.

VITA: It's way out of the way, don't worry. I think maybe take something that's actually called Hot Water Road to Route 44. We may have to backtrack.

MARION: Excuse me, but you're not taking Hot Water Road and you're not taking 44. We were headed for 44. They're turning everyone back. All routes east, west, and north.

NILES: You're joking.

MARION: I'm afraid not. Unless you want to go down to Mexico.

NILES: I would love to go down to Mexico. I would especially adore going down to the Yucatán Peninsula. I unfortunately am going to Phoenix, Arizona.

VITA: We can be late; we're in no rush.

(*The noise of a helicopter approaches, growing deafeningly loud*)

VITA: What on earth?

NILES: What in hell.

VITA: (*Looking out*) Helicopter. Very low. *Very* low.

HELICOPTER: (*From speakers above, a stentorian voice*) The roads are closed. Please stay indoors.

MARION: (*Yelling*) Well, that's a new one.

HELICOPTER: Please stay indoors. The roads are temporarily closed. (*It passes by*)

NILES: Dear Lord, the dust.

VITA: (*Overlapping*) My ears are ringing.

MARION: (*Overlapping*) Do you believe it? "Temporarily closed." The last time they said that, the traffic was rerouted around the area for four days.

NILES: Still, there doesn't seem cause for these alarums and excursions.

MARION: Some of the houses don't have electricity or radios.

ZAP: (*Enters*) You hear that?

MARION: I may never hear another thing, but I heard that.

ZAP: What is that supposed to mean?

MARION: Just a precaution, everything's fine.

ZAP: Sure, sure, we're probably dying here, everything's fine.

MARION: There's no point in getting a stroke.

ZAP: I know, I know. The radio's still saying any minute, so we're cool. It wasn't a plane crash, they're saying it was a truck and something about high winds.

DOHERTY: (*Enters, picking up trash*) Get her to take a little water and slip some broth in when she isn't looking. I don't know. Did you hear that? Aren't they exciting? I threw a rock at one of them, I think they laughed at me. Over the loudspeakers. I'm picking up trash. Where does it come from in a week? On top of everything else, Mrs. Valdez has stopped eating. Says she's going to die. I told her that was certain if she didn't eat. She said she'd lived to be ninety, and that's all she'd planned on.

MARION: What are you doing here? I didn't expect to see you.

DOHERTY: I've changed my schedule. Our little genius is running away. You've settled the estate?

MARION: What with the sale and the transfer of the paintings, I've signed my name in the last two days more than most rock stars.

DOHERTY: Are you all right? You're not, of course, neither am I. I have to ask and you have to say "I'm fine."

MARION: I'm fine.

DOHERTY: As bad as that?

MARION: I'm fine.

DOHERTY: (*Looking out the door*) He's turned around. The little ingrate. Those choppers must have done the trick. He's coming back. Not a word.

VITA: It looks as if we're detained for a few minutes. Is it all right if we wait here?

DOHERTY: Oh, yes. Maria will be very happy. Happy, happy. She always makes refreshments when she sees a car stop, so we'll have a little treat. She loves people, but she's terrified of them. Wouldn't go near one. But this sort of thing makes her day.

MARION: Lucky for her that it happens all the time.

DOHERTY: Marion can tell you. No alarm, no alarm. (*Exits into residence*)

VITA: I'll bring in the hamper and we'll have a sandwich. You haven't eaten a bite.

NILES: I haven't been hungry, I don't know why.

VITA: Even if you don't feel hungry, you should eat. You look terrible.

NILES: Thank you, I'm fine!

ZAP: (*Pill in one hand, thermos in the other*) This ain't cocoa. What is this? I can't take a pill with gin. This is the martinis.

MARION: It's zinc. It's a mineral. Alcohol won't affect that.

ZAP: I'm not talking chemical reaction, I'm talking swallowing. I can't slug back gin like that.

MARION: You don't need that much liquid.

ZAP: You don't. I do. What if that got stuck in there?

MARION: Just work up a mouthful of saliva, then. It's down before you—

ZAP: Oh, fine, I'm dying in the middle of the desert, I'm supposed to work up a load of spit.

MARION: Concentrate. Think of a lemon. A nice . . . tart
. . . juicy . . . sour . . .

ZAP: Come on, what are you trying to do to me. I need a
glassful of water. You know that.

VITA: Apparently there's a faucet out there.

NILES: I wouldn't trust it for drinking. Unless you're des-
perate.

ZAP: Where's the hot chocolate?

MARION: (*Patiently*) You read that chocolate was ninety
percent cholesterol, and cholesterol causes cardiac arrest,
and you said you didn't want me to make hot chocolate
this trip.

ZAP: (*Overlapping from "cardiac"*) It ain't that important,
I won't take it now. It doesn't matter, it's cool. (*To* VITA *and*
NILES) Excuse us, okay? (*To* MARION) I was gonna bring
a soda, it's my own fault.

MARION: It amazes me how you can make a simple thing
like taking a pill into a Rain Dance.

ZAP: (*Serious*) You okay? Something wrong? I'm a little
weird about pills.

MARION: No, I just forget what a baby you are.

ZAP: (*Lighter*) No, now, no. This has nothing to do with
babying myself. This has to do with a basic fear that runs
in my family. My mother had this. This is the fear of
choking. This is just a simple preventative thing that when
you take a few precautions is no problem to anybody. (*To*

VITA *and* NILES) Excuse us, okay? (*Back to* MARION) The way I grew up, you take a pill with one full glass of water.

VITA: Did someone in your family choke?

ZAP: (*Point made*) Never.

VITA: We have some seltzer in the car.

ZAP: No, miss. Don't go to any damn trouble.

VITA: (*Exiting*) It's no damn trouble at all.

ZAP: Why do you always do this? (MARION *is laughing*) The simplest thing and you bring attention to me. You're as bad as my sister. When I was fourteen, we go to a dance, I'm standing outside cruising the chicks, my sister spits on a handkerchief and starts washing my face. Sportswriters all over the country every day eat me for breakfast; I don't need it from my old lady, you know?

MARION: (*Still laughing*) I don't like "old lady," don't say "old lady." It's too close to home. I'll ask Father Doherty if he can get you a glass of water from the kitchen.

ZAP: Fuck it, gimme it, fuck it. I'll drink the gin.

MARION: Not if it's going to be such a problem. She's gone to get a soda, you don't have to.

ZAP: (*Takes the pill, drinks from the thermos, sputters enormously*) Oh, boy. Oh, boy. Oh, wooo! Oh, great. That is one very dry martini. Woooo!

MARION: You okay?

ZAP: (*Red-faced and coughing*) Give me your handkerchief. Oh, boy.

VITA: (*Enters*) Here you go. I'm afraid it's warm.

ZAP: (*Immediately fakes cool*) Oh, thanks, but like I said, everything's cool. No problem.

MARION: Save it. There's a different one every half hour. Packing for a trip is a logistical nightmare.

ZAP: No, that's fine. We're cool. It's down there. It's doing its thing.

VITA: You look the picture of health.

ZAP: I'm healthy, I'm healthy. I'm a physical specimen.

(DON *comes in front door, sees them, turns on his heel and leaves*)

ZAP: Hi.

MARION: Don!

ZAP: Boy oh, boy oh, boy. If we even get out of here alive, this is just great preparation, I'm telling you.

MARION: We'll get there. Please don't work yourself up into a flither.

ZAP: I'm in a flither, I'm in a flither. (*Exits into garden*) It's okay, I like it.

MARION: Total child. My name's Marion Clay.

NILES: Niles Harris; my wife, Vita.

MARION: Pleased to meet you. Under any other circumstances.

VITA: We'll make the best of it. I love him, he reminds me of my brother.

MARION: Salvatore Zappala. Zappy Zappala.

VITA: Is he any good?

MARION: How do you mean?

VITA: Tennis.

MARION: Oh, I think so. A lot of people expect him to go all the way. Unfortunately, he has the worst luck in the world. The last four . . . *four* . . . tournaments he's drawn the eventual winner on the first round.

VITA: Oh, no.

MARION: And all four times he's fought them to a tie-breaker in the last set before he lost. Forget the burning bush, give him a break on the first-round draw. That would be a miracle.

DON: (*Charging back in*) Marion, do you know anything about this?

MARION: What did Arthur say?

DON: Arthur doesn't know his ass.

MARION: Some accident up at Chin Rock mine.

DON: That bastard won't let me go there.

MARION: Don't you have a pass, some sort of ID?

DON: He knows who I am. The son-of-a-bitch can't understand anything except he has orders to stop traffic. I can't get Chin Rock on the phone.

MARION: You can't get anything on the phone.

DON: Was anyone hurt?

MARION: I don't know, love. We were listening on the radio, but they didn't tell us anything. Chin Rock probably owns the radio station. (*To* VITA *and* NILES) Did you meet Don?

NILES: Not formally. Niles Harris; my wife, Vita.

MARION: Don Tabaha.

(*A phone rings in the distance*)

VITA: Do you have a call in?

MARION: No.

DON: I'll get it. (*Exits*)

VITA: (*Jumping up*) That's for us. Well . . .

NILES: This nonsense has us a little—I don't like delays. Ah, well . . . It's cool.

MARION: I know . . . it's cool.

NILES: I meant the temperature, actually.

DON: (*Entering*) You said you're Mrs. Harris?

VITA: Yes. (*To* NILES) Are you okay?

NILES: Fine, fine; briefly.

(VITA *exits*)

DON: Don't tie up that line. They may try to reach me here. Damnit!

MARION: You have Rhode Island plates.

NILES: Providence. The city.

MARION: You're driving to Phoenix?

NILES: Yes. Our first trip West, so we're taking in all the out-of-the-way sights. Hence these interesting local . . . diversions. (*He looks out the window to make sure* VITA *is on the phone, goes to her purse and digs for his Valium*) When I told a colleague of mine we were going out West, he said: "To Las Vegas in a hand basket, I presume." I suppose you had to be there. I was always relating some half-witty anecdote to my class, who stared back vacantly in just that manner.

MARION: You teach, then?

NILES: I taught. Or I lectured. Rather too steadily for thirty years. I'm on a sabbatical that had originally been scheduled for the purpose of writing yet another book, but it will now conform to the ancient Israelite sabbatical in which every seventh year the field was left untilled.

MARION: Ummm. And slaves were released and debts were forgiven.

NILES: Let's hope there's no necessity to go as far as that.

MARION: Were you at work on the great American novel?

NILES: No, no. I would have wanted it to sell. My field was the only somewhat less fictional one of art history.

MARION: And art history sells.

NILES: Like beer at a ball game; you have no idea.

MARION: I do. I own the Clay Gallery in Chicago. I'm Marion Branch. Ernest Branch's wife.

NILES: Ernest Branch!

MARION: The Regional Artist.

NILES: Good Lord, I thought he died.

MARION: He did.

NILES: Oh, forgive me. How tactless of me—

MARION: No, no, my fault—I should have said Ernie used to be my husband—

NILES: No, no, thank you; but in any case, how asinine and rude. Forgive me— (VITA *enters carrying a picnic basket*) Darling, Miss Clay is the wife of the painter Ernest Branch.

VITA: I'm glad to meet you all over again. I liked his work a lot. I have to talk about anything later than the seventeenth century behind Niles's back. I've seen articles about your place. What's it called?

MARION: I'm afraid it's called the Branch Ranch. And there's a sometimes creek that runs through the middle of the property that's called the Branch Branch.

VITA: I didn't realize we were that close to it here.

MARION: Eight miles. There's only sixteen acres, but the buildings are good and the situation is spectacular, of course. One of those private green valleys.

NILES: Everything all right with Phoenix?

VITA: Oh, it's a bother; you don't want to know. His secretary will call us back. She has to get him out of a conference; he'll want to talk to you.

NILES: Absolutely not.

VITA: He'll just want to understand the circumstances of—

NILES: I said no. When have you known me to say no and mean anything other than no. Absolutely not. I've no intention of talking to him.

VITA: Fine. I'll talk to him.

NILES: Admirable.

DOHERTY: (*Backing in, carrying a tray with lemonade and sugar. He is talking to someone inside.* DON *stands*) Well, come in and take a bow. Make an appearance. (*Laughs*) She gets so embarrassed. What did I tell you? (*Sees* DON) Hello, Don. Don't you look surprised to see me. I hear you had a fight with your uncle. (*To* NILES) His uncle goes off into the mountains and yells at the sky for two days when they fight. He comes back so hoarse he can hardly speak. (*To* DON) I see you've packed your knapsack and have your motorbike working again for your getaway. I'm making Saturday evening the Sunday obligation tonight. I re-arranged my schedule so I could see you off.

DON: I didn't see your car.

DOHERTY: No, I parked around back. Aren't I cunning? (*To the others*) Now, Maria has made lemonade. Isn't that musical. (*He passes the glasses around*) Cheers. To Maria.

NILES: No, no, no, don't go to any— I don't really care for lemonade. I always think it's doing something to the enamel on my teeth. Well . . . thank you. That's fine. To—?

MARION: Maria.

DOHERTY: Or maybe we should drink to Don's newfound fortune.

MARION: What fortune?

DON: Skip it.

DOHERTY: Newfound opportunity, then.

DON: If I didn't know better, I'd think you arranged this roadblock.

DOHERTY: The efficacy of prayer? No, nothing this alarming.

MARION: Does Maria have the paper from Gallup? Zap has a match tomorrow. They had the draw this morning.

DOHERTY: (*Trying to remember*) Zap. Zap, zap, zap, zap.

MARION: Never mind, I'll get it. If I don't scare her to death.

DON: I'll get it.

MARION: It won't be in any of the local papers, but it gives me something to do.

DON: Terrific party, Father. You really know how to throw it.

DOHERTY: You'll be back. We should have a nice talk before you leave. (DON *exits into residence*) Young Tabaha is going through his lapsed phase just now.

VITA: He lives here?

DOHERTY: Oh, yes. He's the nephew of our little church mouse, Maria. His mother abandoned him to her sister. Said she had no idea who the father was.

NILES: But the father wasn't Indian?

DOHERTY: We wonder lately if he was even human. (*Offers* VITA *sugar*) Sugar?

VITA: I have honey, thanks.

DOHERTY: This has been Don's playroom since before he could walk. Right up through high school he's done his homework here, invited his friends here, so he's a little possessive about the place. I always had to let him ring the bell. He's had an alarming change of heart since he's been at the medical school. The big city works its wiles, but I'm sure we can set him straight.

NILES: Medical school?

MARION: He's on a full scholarship, of course.

DOHERTY: Always was brilliant, and that's never easy.

MARION: He's interning now. Goes up to the Indian hospital once a week. That's what he always wanted.

DOHERTY: Wonderful to see that. Went about that high with a stethoscope around his neck. A real one, not a toy. No idea where he got it. Dragging to his ankles. Said he'd been working on the reservation. Where you been, Dr. Don? "I been working on the reservation." Now he is. Wonderful to see that. (*Sings*) "I've been working on the reservation . . ."

MARION: He should be at Chin Rock—that dope Arthur wouldn't let him through.

DOHERTY: Before he heard about Chin Rock he was trying to run away, so I'm grateful for Arthur.

VITA: Oh, yes. I was talking to Phoenix, and I'm afraid we're international news. This is the third time something's gone wrong at the Chin Rock mine.

NILES: What, dear God, is the Chin Rock mine?

MARION and DOHERTY: Uranium.

NILES: Oh, lovely. You've known that all along?

VITA: We learn these little things one at a time.

MARION: If they don't have us on the road in ten minutes, this is going to cost me a thousand bucks to charter a plane.

VITA: At the risk of being an alarmist, I heard them say it might be an hour or more before the highway is reopened. (*To* NILES) Don't pace.

NILES: Why ever not? It seems the perfect physical expression of the situation. One suddenly understands polar bears.

VITA: Are you all right?

NILES: Oh, my dear, of course I am. There's no need to feel my forehead, I'm fine.

VITA: I'm not used to all this unfocused energy.

NILES: I've never been what one might describe as lethargic.

VITA: No, one would have described you as focused.

NILES: Very well, *do* feel my forehead. (*As she does, he smiles forbearingly*) We must look a couple of complete asses, Mr. Zappala and I. You baby us too much, as he said.

VITA: You're burning up. Are you coming down with something?

NILES: (*Takes off jacket*) Lord, I'm perspiring like a— something that perspires. Heavily. Ah, well . . .

MARION: I should warn you, it doesn't pay to get sick in this country. There isn't a doctor within eighty miles.

DOHERTY: And Don is a genius, but I wouldn't give you a nickel for his bedside manner.

NILES: No, no, quite the contrary. I'm just recuperating from the effects of a—traumatic nervous breakthrough.

MARION: When do you get back to the college?

NILES: No, no, no, I've quite burned my bridges. I won't be going back to the college.

DOHERTY: You're a professor, that explains it.

MARION: Art history.

NILES: I used to be a professor, and I used to be an author. But fortunately I experienced what you might call a crisis of faith, or a disturbance in my willful suspension of disbelief that allowed me to see what I had done for what it was. You see, while framing the schema of my new book, I made the tactical error of rereading my other books.

MARION: Oh, no.

NILES: I'm afraid so. They are, of course, the authoritative statement on the subject. Both in style and in fact.

MARION: I remember.

NILES: Of course you'd be familiar with them.

MARION: A long time ago.

NILES: Let's not discuss how long ago.

MARION: That's a deal.

NILES: Well, Miss Clay, to every didactic, authoritative sentence I had written, I said: "Yes, of course, and exactly the opposite could be as true." Or: "Whereas we have assumed the artistic expression of a culture was the mirror of the people's soul, and that from that mirror we can posit an aesthetic for our own enlightenment—it is also possible that the expression of an artist tells us nothing whatever about the people and from it we can posit—nothing."

MARION: I *think* I followed that.

VITA: There'll be a quiz later.

NILES: Never again, never again. All I said, really, was that I reread the three books that I had written and didn't believe a word of them. Not one. So, naturally, I asked myself what on earth I had been doing for thirty years, and woke up one morning to discover that I suspected that I had been bought.

VITA: Not bought.

NILES: Worse. That I had been subtly conscripted as part of that elite corps who have been given the necessary task of "breaking the bronco from dancing." Or brainwashing the little bastards.

VITA: Not that the little so-and-sos appreciated what you were telling them.

NILES: I have the comfort of knowing that I made my statement.

VITA: Oh, and vividly. He has rather a flair for the dramatic.

MARION: We hardly noticed.

DOHERTY: Not at all.

NILES: (*Laughs*) Oh, dear, if I say so myself, I was magnificent.

VITA: Three weeks before the term final, he burst into his classroom—

NILES: Certainly not. I walked majestically and deliberately to my desk and did not sit down.

VITA: And announced to his class that the course was useless.

NILES: I said it was something akin to buffalo chips.

VITA: —took his three published books from his briefcase and ripped them in half.

NILES: And flung them in the air. I was exalted. *The Imagination of Ancient Greece.* (*Rips in half*) There! to *The Imagination of Ancient Greece.* I know nothing about it, and neither does anyone else. Oh, it was wonderful.

VITA: And in his exaltation he had mislaid his glasses, so on his way to class he drove the car straight across the iris bed at the entrance to the college.

NILES: I was fired with the message of truth.

VITA: And coming back he drove the shortest route to the street, which was directly across the badminton court.

NILES: *Nolo contendere.*

VITA: Then he stopped off to have a celebratory drink, and he doesn't drink. It's a miracle you got home. God protects drunkards and little children, both of which would cover him.

DOHERTY: That's blasphemy, of course.

NILES: Unfortunately, several of my students are reactionary little—

VITA: Nerds.

NILES: And their parents are worse, and they are suing the college.

VITA: Our class would have stood up and cheered. Carried you over our heads about the corridors.

NILES: Your class was unruly, unwashed, and very nearly undressed. It's one of my most cherished memories.

MARION: You were a student of his?

VITA: That's where we met.

NILES: A-minus, and she had the nerve to come to my office to discuss the minus.

VITA: That wasn't the reason I came to your office. That was just the excuse.

NILES: Do you mean that after nine years of marriage I discover that you deliberately contrived—

VITA: Anyway. The professors convened with the provost. All except Whittington . . .

NILES: . . . head of the botany department . . .

VITA: . . . who was still saying: "Look what that brute's done to my iris bed!"

NILES: And I was completely exonerated. Enough, now.

VITA: Unfortunately, the Board of Governors was not quite so obliging.

NILES: Certainly not. They're capable of recognizing sick behavior when they see it. Enough now. We're telling stories out of school.

MARION: Do you care?

NILES: Not a fig.

MARION: Imagine Ernie ripping up his life's work.

NILES: Another fig for my life's work.

MARION: I might pace back and forth, after something like that.

DOHERTY: But you experienced a disturbance in your willful suspension of disbelief.

NILES: Coleridge had it as "willing," I believe.

DOHERTY: Wonderful phrase. I don't think I'd like the experience. That would be a real doozer.

NILES: Isn't that a doozer? Well, better now, on only slightly the downside of the prime of life than on . . . say . . . one's deathbed. That *would* be a doozer. (*Old voice*) Oh, my God, I've just realized that I'm full of shit.

VITA: (*Offers him lemonade*) Why don't you sit and join us, Niles.

NILES: Thanks, no, darling. I don't like lemonade. I'm sorry, it's probably fine as lemonade goes, but—why am I trying to be nice? Do you suppose I'm growing considerate in my old age?

VITA: I doubt it.

NILES: Sorry about the profanity. I don't usually.

DOHERTY: No, no. The scatological comment was very amusing. "Oh, my God, I've just realized I'm full of beans" doesn't have the same ring. The "Oh, my God" was unnecessary, but I never scold about that sort of thing.

DON: (*Offstage, shouting in Navaho. Enters, sees* MARION) Oh, damnit. (*Exits back into the residence*)

DOHERTY: Something about money. It usually is lately. Did you have violent arguments with your parents over money when you were young?

NILES: No.

VITA: Yes.

MARION: Yes.

DOHERTY: So did I.

DON: (*Enters with newspaper*) Here's the paper. It's not going to be in it. (*He goes out*)

MARION: I know, I know.

VITA: (*Looking off after* DON) A brilliant doctor, hm? Well, if you say so.

MARION: Ernie painted him. It's the only painting I know I'm going to keep. It's one of the best things he did.

DOHERTY: Don pretended to hate Ernie, but he didn't, really.

MARION: I know. That's exactly what Ernie painted. The smugness, the fear, the belligerence, the uncertainty, the superiority, the distrust of the painter, the love. All staring right out at you. It's beautiful.

(ZAP *enters, wearing earphones*)

DOHERTY: You're Zap. I knew I knew Zap. Hello, Zap.

ZAP: Hi.

DOHERTY: Zap, zap, zap, zap, zap.

ZAP: I'm probably dying here. My skin is probably falling off. I'm getting the report here.

MARION: Zap, you did not dig through the suitcase for the radio. I spent two hours organizing— (ZAP *removes earphones to hear*) —well—good boy!

(DON *enters*)

ZAP: Hi.

DON: What's up?

MARION: (*Looking at the dust on the seat of Don's pants*) Look at you. (*She brushes dust off him*)

DON: Come on, Marion. Zap's your boytoy, I'm not your boytoy.

ZAP: (*To* DON) Hey, Doctor, you go to New York, you go down to the Village, you dress like that, you'll pick up a lot of Jewish girls.

MARION: Have you two ever actually been introduced?

ZAP: Yeah, I know him, he's "Brave with Arrow." She's got you hanging over her fireplace in Lake Forest. Least he's not in the room where we eat, right?

DON: What's up?

ZAP: It ain't good at all. You don't want to know. A guy's already died.

DON: Who?

DOHERTY: Who?

ZAP: Some Indian. They're not releasing the name till they tell the family. Boy, that gives me the crawlies.

NILES: Died?

ZAP: What's yellow cake?

DOHERTY: Where was this?

ZAP: Up at the Chin Rock mine. It's a mess. This truck was supposed to be being loaded and instead it backed up over the containers and they busted, and the wind blew all this yellow cake stuff all over the guys that were loading it. Those helicopters were coming to take the guys who are still alive to the hospital in Los Alamos.

MARION: Up from White Sands. Wouldn't you know they'd get into the act.

VITA: Yellow cake is pure uranium, refined at the mill. That's from my protesting days.

ZAP: How far away is that Chin Rock mine?

DOHERTY: Twenty miles? Thirty miles?

MARION: Twenty miles as the buzzard flies.

ZAP: What really gripes you, though—what they're saying is, anybody not in the immediate area won't get sick for about twelve years.

DOHERTY: Minor levels, minor levels.

NILES: Don't panic the populus.

ZAP: You get the picture, twelve years from now you're walking down the street, you're feeling great, all of a sudden you're a spot on the sidewalk.

(Pause. They look to DOHERTY, *who has his fingers pressed to his forehead, his eyes closed. His lips are moving. He prays silently. After a moment he crosses himself, looks up, smiles.* VITA *moves to a window, looking out)*

VITA: I keep envisioning us all being slowly covered with Chin Rock ash. Like the people of Pompeii. A thousand years from now this will be an archaeological site with markers saying: This is a professor, this is his wife, this is a hopeful tennis player, with his rackets.

ZAP: Come on.

DOHERTY: No, no, it sounds very minor. We're not that close. People all over the country are going to be terribly disappointed. They'd rather have a big gaudy cataclysm. They've been preparing themselves for years.

VITA: Look at it. It looks so clean and immutable.

DOHERTY: No, no, quite mutable. Mute, mute, mute. Those solid-looking mountains, if you tried to climb them, would mute right out from under your foot.

VITA: I keep looking for an eagle. Can they really pick up children and fly off with them? Would that be too scary?

NILES: She doesn't mean that literally. Vita writes stories for children.

DOHERTY: You do? Wonderful.

VITA: They're nothing. They only sell because I have a very clever partner who does the illustrations. In spite of all this, I envy anyone who has a place here.

MARION: You either love it or you hate it. I sold it.

VITA: Oh, no.

MARION: I couldn't hack it. The first freezing night I spent here I woke up to Ernie carrying a rattlesnake through the bedroom at the end of a pair of fireplace tongs. They come in to warm themselves on the hearth.

NILES: We learn these little things one at a time.

MARION: He throws them back over the fence. To grow, I suppose. The romanticism completely escapes me. I think he'd read Georgia O'Keeffe did that. I'm sorry. I left without packing a bag. Drove to Chicago before I called him.

NILES: He wasn't a complete hermit, then. He had a phone.

MARION: Oh, by the swimming pool. And a large house and a large studio and a salon with a gaggle of fawning admirers.

NILES: It can't be easy being an artist today.

MARION: Nothing simpler, believe me.

DOHERTY: I'm going to hate to see you go. Isn't that what we're supposed to say? But I will. Marion used to spend a month here in the summer and a month in the winter.

MARION: Shaking my shoes out every morning in case a scorpion had holed up inside during the night.

DOHERTY: Very possible, of course, very possible. But I wouldn't leave here. They'd have to blast me out.

VITA: You don't have a choice, do you? Aren't you assigned?

DOHERTY: Yes, yes, we're sent. We don't just move where we'd like. They sent me all the way from Worcester, Mass. But they'd have to drag me away. Wild horses. (*Singsong*) "Wild, wild horses couldn't drag me away." Now, why is that? It isn't healthy for me. Why would I fight for my inch of land to the bitter end? The grave of my dear little daughter who died that first hard winter is definitely not out on the hill behind the old corral. My father and his father before him never laid eyes on the place. Ah, well . . . Silly Billy. (*To* MARION) Do you miss him? I miss him terribly. (*Beat*) I miss our Sunday afternoons. Ernie used to come here after his struggles at the studio. Silly Ernie.

He had to get away from all those people. I think he only
invited them to come so he'd have someone to get away
from. He'd steal an hour away, and I'd steal an hour away.
We sat out back under Maria's arbor. He'd drink wine and
I'd drink tea, and we both got drunk. I miss all that. I
don't sit there anymore. He liked his friends at a little distance, didn't he? Not in a position to grab anything. Like
some of the limelight. Sunday afternoons.

ZAP: Let up, okay?

MARION: (*With energy, thrusts paper aside*) There's nothing in the paper, of course. They've had the draw hours ago.
The only thing to do is call San Diego and get it over the
phone.

ZAP: You okay?

DOHERTY: Was I being insensitive?

MARION: No, I need something to do.

ZAP: You want me to call?

MARION: I want me to call. Excuse me. (*Exits*)

DOHERTY: Button my lip.

ZAP: Yeah, well, you get used to talking to yourself, you
sorta just talk to yourself if someone's there to listen or not,
you know?

DOHERTY: I know, I know. Silly Billy. Button my lip, button
my lip.

ZAP: It ain't too easy on her coming back down here. I'll

ask her to marry me again. I ask her every coupla days. She always gets a good laugh outta that.

VITA: (*To* DON) Scorpions aren't that dangerous, are they? I think I've read that.

DON: How would I know?

VITA: There's no reason you should. I thought you might. When do you finish your internship?

NILES: We've been talking about you behind your back, Doctor.

DOHERTY: No, Don has decided he doesn't want to be a doctor anymore. So he won't have to finish his internship now. (DON *looks at him*) You didn't know I found out, did you? (*He exits through the front door*)

VITA: Why wouldn't you finish your internship? I thought you were doing so well.

DON: (*Beat*) There's a species of scorpion in Mexico that's been known to be fatal to infants. It wouldn't seriously harm an adult.

ZAP: Scorpions. Oh, man.

DON: The tarantula's the same, rarely fatal. Unless the bite gets infected with gangrene.

ZAP: Gangrene?

DON: But that could happen from—tennis elbow.

VITA: I thought tarantulas were deadly.

DON: White wives' tale. Sorry.

ZAP: You got those here?

DON: White wives? Not many.

ZAP: Tarantulas!

DON: Tarantulas, oh. Pick up a rock. Little ones; six inches across.

ZAP: Oh, give me a break.

DON: Won't hurt you. The coral snake is really deadly, though. We understand you don't feel the bite.

VITA: (*In mock awe*) You don't feel the bite?

DON: You just start feeling numb around the area; then a paralysis starts to set in—

ZAP: No, no, no, no. Don't talk symptoms. I can't hear symptoms. This is truly. I can't hear that.

VITA: Snakebite, Zappy. Snakebite.

ZAP: I can't hear symptoms without getting it. I know. This has happened.

DON: With snakebite it usually requires the snake.

ZAP: Not with me it don't require no snake.

NILES: They're putting you on.

ZAP: Yeah, well, he's putting me on, but he isn't making it up.

DON: I tell you, Zappy, it's a jungle out there in the desert.

DOHERTY: (*Enters behind* ZAP. ZAP *jumps a foot*) No alarm, no alarm.

(MARION *re-enters*)

ZAP: They got the draw?

MARION: Lines are busy. I'll try in a minute.

VITA: So. Why aren't you going to finish your internship and be a doctor?

MARION: What? That's news to me.

DON: Dr. Lindermann has asked me to join his cancer research team at Berkeley.

MARION: Oh, bullshit. Excuse me.

DOHERTY: (*Mumbled*) Under the circumstances . . .

VITA: How did you get into cancer research? Not that I know anything about it.

DON: The last year or so I've been interested in gene structure, protein production, cellular experiments.

VITA: Is that like DNA?

DON: Like that.

DOHERTY: My goodness.

DON: There are some fairly complicated machines and equipment involved that I seem to understand better than some.

MARION: I'm sure, but I thought you turned them down. You talked to Ernie about it.

DOHERTY: Oh, that's last year's news. That was a lab in Pittsburgh. But those poor devils toil day and night for little reward. Dr. Don got very indignant and told them— quite movingly I thought, Don—that he must follow his calling and minister to his own people.

MARION: The Indian on the reservation doesn't respond well to outsiders.

DON: You've deliberately misunderstood everything I've said for the last two years.

DOHERTY: Nothing you've said has made sense. But the lure of Dr. Noah Lindermann is not to be sneezed at. One of those charismatic "leaders of his field," always being interviewed on TV.

VITA: We've met him. I think we were less than impressed.

NILES: To say the least.

DOHERTY: Well, he's been at the college for the last three months. But now the Famous Man is returning to his research project and luring away his brightest star with the offer of an astronomical salary in a glamorous position.

DON: (*Very angry*) If I were interested in being glamorous

and making money, I could stay right here and be glamorous as hell and rake it in by the kilo. What do you think, Marion? Maybe I should hang up my shingle as the half-breed podiatrist. All those seven-foot Texans in Santa Fe walking around in their pointy boots. Their toes must be killing them.

MARION: Mine too, but I'm not sure I'd put my feet in your hands.

DOHERTY: Neither would they.

DON: And with this sun they'll need a dermatologist.

DOHERTY: (*To* DON) Tell us about the respiratory disease among the Navaho mine workers.

DON: And a handsome young endocrinologist could make a killing.

DOHERTY: (*Rather heated*) Talk to us about the rate of birth defects on the reservation.

DON: And there's a pretty penny here for a proctologist.

DOHERTY: I've never seen a pretty penny.

DON: And the entire desert is weeping for an anaesthesiologist. I know I am.

DOHERTY: I know I am.

MARION: Wasn't that fun. Only now you're both hyperventilating.

DON: Not me.

VITA: Why would there be a higher rate of birth defects on the reservation than there would be in the rest of the area?

MARION: They live right in the middle of the uranium mines.

DOHERTY: Most of the men work there.

DON: (*Still quite angry*) Congenital anomalies, lung cancer, tuberculosis, chromosomal aberrations, sperm morphological distortion—begins to get scary, doesn't it?

VITA: I can see why Father Doherty doesn't want to lose you.

DON: I'm just getting started, honey. Kidney disease, glaucoma, and there's no time for one person in a hundred years to begin to correct a millennium of genetic neglect.

VITA: So you just wave goodbye to it.

DON: In abject humiliation, yes.

VITA: You think that's all just romantic folly now?

DON: No, darlin', I think that is a deep and abiding tragedy.

NILES: I would have welcomed the idea that you were a practicing radiologist.

DON: We're not so skittish about radiation as you are. Having been forced to live with it all our lives.

NILES: Well, you won't be any longer.

DON: Who put a straw up your butt?

NILES: I would have thought there would have been a need on the reservation for a nutritionist.

DON: There is, Doctor.

NILES: Professor. A pediatrician.

DON: There is, Doctor.

NILES: Then I guess I miss the point of your little sally.

DON: You can't imagine.

NILES: I can imagine the horrors of the ninth circle, but if you mean it's ignorant speculation, you're quite right.

DON: (*Very hard*) There is no *time*, Doctor. No time for any of it.

NILES: (*Loud*) I'm never addressed as doctor, and I've recently turned in my badge. "Professor" was preferred to "doctor," but I didn't insist on it. (DOHERTY *stands*) I'm sorry. I'm being snide and I don't know why. My wife and I are accustomed to being mildly insulted by students. I'm not myself, as I said. And whoever I am, I seem to have little control of him.

VITA: You're fine.

MARION: Zappy could give you one of his Valiums. Goodness knows, he has them to spare.

VITA: I don't think Dr. Singer believes in tranquillizers.

NILES: Please!

DON: Singer's!

VITA: What?

NILES: Really!

VITA: What?

DON: Well, goddamn. No wonder he's off the wall. He's on his way to the nuthouse.

NILES: Nothing of the kind.

DON: Hold on to your tranquillizers, Zappy; he's so doped up now he's not responsible for anything he's said all afternoon.

NILES: (*Overlapping*) I'm just constitutionally ill-equipped for changes in plans. Surprises annoy me. And though the lessons in local ophiology and arachnology are diverting, I'm sure you'll understand.

DOHERTY: (*Overlapping*) Pooh, pooh, pooh, pooh. Winnie the Pooh. Pooh out of the bag. (*To* DON) Settle down now. Nothing to be embarrassed about. We know all about Doc Singer.

DON: Ernie and his crowd knew every expensive psychiatric hangout in the West.

NILES: Not at all, not at all.

DON: He's going off to be shock-treated or warm-bathed . . .

NILES: I won't be shock-treated—I won't be warm-bathed—

DOHERTY: We've seen it a hundred times. You'll come back placid as a cow.

NILES: Not at all. (*To* VITA) You see what silliness you started?

MARION: It costs a fortune, I hope you realize that.

NILES: We know, of course, that it's exorbitant— (*Sighs*) Oh, well.

VITA: (*Pause*) The pretense that this was a vacation was beginning to wear a little thin.

NILES: Especially between the two of us, yes. I only agreed to go to such a ridiculous high-class funny farm to humor the Board of Governors of the college. They're picking up the tab, of course. They feel it will appease the parents if they can tell them I've had a complete collapse.

ZAP: Don't take the medicine if you don't need it.

MARION: Cool it, Zap.

NILES: Well, actually, Zappy, two months ago I was fabulously healthy in mind and limb. But since we've had the appointment I've prepared myself for the place by becoming a total basket case. I think my mind has a natural aversion to wasting money.

ZAP: Sure.

DOHERTY: Well, good. You'll be in wonderful hands. Best in the West, best in the West. Don is a little skeptical about that sort of place, but that's to be expected.

DON: Out of my field. Dude-ranch psychiatric hospitals are not the Indian's bag.

NILES: It sounds like the Indian's bag is out of your field now.

DON: Enough, okay?

DOHERTY: It's best never to look back, Don. Don't you agree, Professor?

NILES: I wouldn't know.

DOHERTY: You're running away from school, Don is running away from school.

DON: I'm running away from nothing.

NILES: As the young man said, I know nothing about what he's running from.

DON: No, and you're damn well not likely to. Working in your ivy-covered ivory towers back East.

NILES: Oh, hardly. Ivory towers?

DON: The matrons and the patrons who go to Singer's usually fly straight from their penthouses to the padded cells without touching down. They don't usually drive to the loony bin through the wilderness. It's very sporting of you to take a tour through the real world. I hope you learn a lot.

NILES: The real world, the real world, dear Lord. I thought I'd heard the last of the real world. And certainly the idea that academics know nothing of the real world. (*To* VITA) We used to have wonderful talks about the real world, re-

member? In your class? (*To* DON) Begging to differ with
you, the real world has come slouching into my room hourly
for thirty years. The real world is too much with me. I would
expect the young today to see things more clearly. They
certainly clamor more loudly. But it appears youth wears
blinders. Endemically, or, "it comes with the territory."

DON: You don't have to translate endemic. I know the mean-
ing of endemic. It comes with the territory.

NILES: It would. But you appear as blind to the fact of
school life around you as I was at your age. I'm not surprised, I am disappointed.

VITA: Darling.

DON: You're full of it, too.

NILES: Oh, completely, but by all that's holy, man, open
your eyes.

VITA: Don't get upset.

NILES: I am not upset. I am strident and overbearing.

VITA: And a touch irrational—

NILES: This young person is justifiably sickened by the effete
performance of professors of my ilk—

VITA: No one is quite like you, I'm sure.

NILES: Oh, let us hope. No, people are snowflakes; there's
none quite like any. I'm sure there is no comparison to the
deprivation you have lived with and are running from, but
the fact is that the ivory tower is a bloody shambles. How

can you be in school and not know that? The fact of the graceless routine of my life in academe is being awakened at three in the morning, called to the village morgue to identify the mutilated and alcohol-sodden corpse of the victim of a car crash. The fact is—let go of me—is having the brightest light of my fraudulent teaching career quench itself by jumping off the bridge into the bay because in your enlightened age of sexual permissiveness, he was afraid he was sexually deviant. (*Mumbles*) Ivory tower . . . There have been, in fact, seven suicides in the past ten years; in fact, one third of my class each year, and of yours, I'm sure, if you had bothered to look around you, burn themselves out on drugs and overwork and exposure to the pressures of academic life, and are unable to return, probably to their everlasting benefit, if they knew it. Dear God, how can any-one with eyes (VITA *touches his arm*) —stop that, please— think that we are out of touch with the real world. If that's the real world, I beg to plead very familiar with the real world, thank you. The calumny, Lord! (VITA *takes hold of his arm*) Stop touching me, please! What are you trying to do? Make it better? It will not be better, thank you! I won't embarrass you again. You won't have to endure that again. I wish in God's name the door to this building weren't so heavy, so I could slam it. (*He strides out the front door*)

VITA: Niles, don't go out there! I'd better—well, I'd better not, is what I'd better. He'll walk around. He's been getting very—lately—irrational. (*To* DON) Still, it was unnecessary for you to goad him like that. He's unwell physically as well as— I'm sorry.

(*Helicopters heard overhead*)

DOHERTY: They must be taking the injured mine workers to the hospital in Los Alamos. My goodness, what a racket. Our poor little church mouse, Maria, must be under the bed.

I must say, when she called me this morning, it was a wonderfully comic picture. I don't want to make fun, but she's afraid of being electrocuted by the telephone instrument and won't even go near it. Yells and jumps when it rings. Imagine her even getting through to me. The Archangel Gabriel must have intervened for her. She said: "You must come immediately, Father, our doctor is running away." And you almost did. (*Pause*) You used to come to me and say: "It's all so impossible. I don't know if I'll ever do anything right." And I said you would. And here Dr. Lindermann has presented you with such a golden opportunity to make something of yourself.

DON: What do you know about it?

DOHERTY: Oh, pooh. What do I know? I never know anything.

DON: I can't talk to you.

DOHERTY: You try. (DON *exits to parking lot. To* MARION) Is he going to his bike?

MARION: No, he's charging straight down the road.

DOHERTY: Good. Zappy, take these. (*Throws a set of keys to* ZAP)

ZAP: What are they?

DOHERTY: Just hide them and don't tell me where.

(ZAP *exits into garden*)

MARION: You ought to be ashamed of yourself.

DOHERTY: Well, I'm not. Not a bit. (*He turns to* VITA)

VITA: I thought he'd be all right if I came with him. He's just been getting worse. Well, he'll be fine.

DOHERTY: Oh, yes. Quite possible. Always possible.

VITA: I'm kind of at the end of my tether here.

DOHERTY: Why don't we talk?

VITA: No, thank you.

DOHERTY: You sure?

VITA: Thank you.

MARION: I'm going to call San Diego again. (*Exits*)

DOHERTY: Yes, yes, yes. Back to work, back to work. Everybody back to the salt mines. (*Sings*) "I've been working on the reservation . . . All the livelong day . . ." (*He exits into the residence.*)

VITA *folds Niles's jacket, holding it on her arm. She turns to the front door, to the garden. A second helicopter goes over, higher, the sound farther away. She looks up and then slowly turns to look at the altar. She stands facing the altar, her back to us.*

Act Two

Half an hour later. ZAP *is lying on the floor, listening to his headset.* FATHER DOHERTY *is at the altar, kneeling. After a moment* VITA *comes in from the garden. The priest rises. He might speak a little less brightly in this act.*

VITA: Don't let me disturb you.

DOHERTY: No, no, impossible. You can't disturb me. I'm full up. I was just asking for the usual. Nothing special. Step up to the altar and say, Give me the usual . . .

VITA: What would that be?

DOHERTY: Oh . . . courage, perseverance, strength.

VITA: Make it a double.

DOHERTY: Oh, I'm sure. After the sun goes down, it gets beautifully cool here. Nights are lovely.

VITA: We spent last night outside Clovis, I know. I hadn't seen stars before. It's the first time I'd had the feeling that the earth was a planet moving through a galaxy of stars. Niles came back to the car and picked up his hat, so he isn't completely irrational.

DOHERTY: So I saw.

ZAP: (*Flat on his back*) That's it. Interstate 40 is definitely moving now. Everything's under control down there. Up here they're still saying eight o'clock, so we're cool. (*Rising*) Who am I talking to? Where is everybody?

VITA: Marion is calling about your schedule again. She was talking to someone, so she seems to have got through.

ZAP: I don't want to know. I know already. I can't talk about it; I want to hear this.

VITA: What are they saying now?

ZAP: (*Earphones off*) What?

VITA: What's the radio saying, now?

ZAP: No, this is the Moody Blues. (*Earphones back on, he stretches back out on the floor*)

DOHERTY: Moody Blues. I hear all those in the car. They're good company, very cheering.

VITA: You drive a lot?

DOHERTY: Oh, yes. All my missions are thirty or forty miles apart. Saturday night at one mission, back to my own at Dry Lake for seven o'clock Sunday Mass, eleven o'clock here, four p.m. at a grammar school assembly hall. I carry a portable altar. And back to Dry Lake for Mass at eight o'clock Sunday night. Little Santa Clara has the Sunday obligation on Wednesday.

VITA: How many are there in your congregation?

DOHERTY: Very good, I think. Most of them are fifteen . . . twenty.

VITA: (*Looking out*) Mr. Tabaha is sitting on his motorcycle all slumped over, his head down, looking into the dust. He looks like an updating of the painting "End of the Trail."

DOHERTY: Yes. This little show of power has interrupted everyone's plans. "Tabaha," "by the river"; that's Navaho for "by the river." I wonder which one? The young miner who died at the Chin Rock mine was twenty-three. His wife is eight months' pregnant with their first child. Four others are ill. I listened on Zappy's headset. Very interesting apparatus. Occupational hazard they're calling it. A uranium mine is no different from a coal mine; coal dust, they're saying. Each is a slow, painful death, they say. But then what isn't? Courage, strength, and perseverance. Moody Blues. Blue, blue, blues.

VITA: What time is Mass?

DOHERTY: Eight.

VITA: If we're still here, I'd like to see the service.

DOHERTY: No, no, nothing to see. I'm afraid there isn't anything to watch. Not even picturesque, I don't imagine. Twelve, fifteen stoic Navahos shuffle in, kneel, I mumble sincerely, they mumble sincerely, and they shuffle out. Nothing to see. Nothing on their faces, probably nothing on mine. In and out. Shuffle—shuffle.

VITA: It must mean something to them, though. And to you.

DOHERTY: Oh, it's what we live for, but there's nothing to see. You're welcome to stay, but you'll be on the road.

They'll get all this cleared up, they'll have a good cover-up story by tomorrow. Bad publicity for the mines if they don't, and the mines are already complaining that the price of uranium has dropped thirty percent in the last ten years. Must be the only price that has. No, you'll be on the road. On the trail by then. Living your life.

MARION: (*Entering*) What are they saying?

ZAP: Hi—

VITA: They're playing the Moody Blues, so it can't be all bad. Interstate 40 is moving. We'll be okay soon. You get through?

MARION: I was calling for a plane. They're ready when we are.

DOHERTY: I-40. Used to be Route 66. I think they do those things deliberately. Don't want us to get too attached to anything.

VITA: Probably just as well.

DOHERTY: Oh, yes. I don't have energy for tonight, not what I'd like to have, but whoever has what he'd like to have. (*Exits to residence*)

MARION: I broke every damn nail I own. Oh, boy. I sound like Zap. The last three days I've been showing a crew of blithely incompetent Indian carpenters how to crate paintings.

VITA: No fun, I'd imagine.

MARION: I shouldn't try; they drive me—oh, well. They

would have done fine left on their own if I hadn't kept
butting in. They were slow, I was nervous, and you've never
seen canvases that size. He had the good sense to leave the
pots to a museum in Albuquerque. And don't think they
weren't Johnny-on-the-spot. Labeling and wrapping and
generally being underfoot— Oh, well, I suppose I should be
grateful . . .

VITA: Are you taking the furniture? I was remembering the
pictures I saw in *Architectural Digest*.

MARION: The rugs and Savonarola chairs and the Mexican
refectory tables? No, thank God, everything was sold with
the buildings. It looks very good here, but for Lake Forest
it's much too "Goodbye, Old Paint, I'm Leaving Cheyenne."
It's more the trauma of seeing the place in such a shambles
than anything.

VITA: I hate moving, breaking up households.

MARION: It's the worst, isn't it?

VITA: All us kids came back to help Mom sort through the
years of mementos when Dad died.

MARION: Oh, thank God, I was spared that. Ernie wasn't a
hoarder.

VITA: Dad kept everything. His dad's cavalry sword from
the First World War. Old ribbons from high school track
meets, his own Second World War stuff—snapshots of D-
day. We even found an old Western saddle stashed away.
He had some secret cowboy fantasy maybe. I made a few
calls. Local preservation societies. It wasn't like he was
famous. Small-town lawyer, state assemblyman, respected
family man. Good money, well-meaning, who cares?

MARION: What did you do with it all?

VITA: Mom took a few things, we all took something, and we burned the rest. Soon as it was gone I felt I'd broken a law. All that crap belonged to the race, not to me. Every scrap should be stored somewhere. You never know which one shard left unburned would tell the tale.

MARION: I expected it to be morbid: going through the studio, looking back over all the paintings, getting them ready for a retrospective. It didn't happen. I hadn't seen most of them in years. It turned out to be very exciting. I sat in the middle of the studio with all the paintings around me. It was like a big blowout with a lot of old friends. I wanted Ernie to be there so I could congratulate him. Even Zap felt it. It's going to be an important show.

VITA: Where are they going?

MARION: Open in Chicago—

VITA: At your gallery.

MARION: At the Art Institute of Chicago. He always wanted that. The bastards had to wait for him to kick off before they gave it to him.

VITA: I imagine he knew it would happen eventually.

MARION: On good days. Then go from Chicago to Denver, then Los Angeles, Dallas, probably not New York. Maybe a few other places. They're all designated for different museums after that. That'll be the hard part, seeing the collection broken up. But it's what he wanted. (*She is trying not to cry*)

VITA: I'll have to see it.

MARION: Try to catch it. (*Moving to the window*) The radio said soon, you said? I think the professor has cooled down a bit. Looks like he might be wandering this way.

VITA: Good. Did Zappy know him?

MARION: Ernie? Yeah. They got along. Ernie was working rather furiously the last few years. He felt better if I had a project. They got along. It's been good for me, it was good for Ernie. Maybe it hasn't been completely fair to Zappy. He gets a little confused. Father Doherty thinks we should "sanctify our relationship" now. I think not. I'll be there 'til he needs something else. So we do learn from our— Zappy, are you hearing this?

ZAP: Sure.

MARION: I forgot you were there, creep.

ZAP: Yeah, I got that problem. You ready to hit the road?

MARION: Soon as it's open.

ZAP: You are getting so weepy, you know? The last week you can't talk about me, you can't talk about Ernie, she can't talk about tumbleweed without the faucet. Yesterday she was crying over the damn sunset.

MARION: Shut up.

ZAP: I can't wait to get you out of here. Get you bossing everybody around again.

MARION: It can't be too soon. (*As* NILES *enters*) Well.

ZAP: Hi!

NILES: (*Tapping his hat*) Don't I look jaunty?

VITA: Almost.

NILES: Forgive me for that astonishing exhibition. I have no idea what causes those—

VITA: (*Overlapping*) No, I'm sorry if I blurted out something you would rather have left as just between ourselves—

NILES: (*Overlapping*) Of course not, what care I? There's no explanation except petulant infantilism—

VITA: We could move the car into the shade now.

NILES: No, darling. I needn't be ostracized to the car. I've walked myself to a frazzle and feel I'm almost fit for social intercourse. (*As* DON *enters*) Dr. Tabaha, I want to apologize for my spectacularly tasteless attack. Nothing personal, believe me. (*Pause*) And you say . . .

DON: No, I just can't deal with Father Doherty. He likes to stir everyone up with his "Don't you think, Don?" and "Wouldn't you agree, Professor?" Anyway, it's interesting to see someone freak out for a change.

ZAP: You like that, I'll take you to my house sometime.

NILES: Freak out. I think that characterizes it perfectly. Walking around out there, I've never felt so twitchy in my life. Aside from knowing that I'm exposing myself to terminal radiation poisoning, I keep thinking enormous ants are going to come up over the hill. Giant spiders. Great amorphous blobs slithering across the sands.

ZAP: Come on.

NILES: I know, but my whole understanding of—or mis-understanding of—nuclear—ah—

VITA: —little nuclear emergencies—

NILES: —emergencies comes from 1950s movies on the Late Show. I suffer from that sci-fi brain damage peculiar to the chronic insomniac.

ZAP: No way, I'm really chicken-livered, you know? Even when I was a kid, any picture the title was in shaky letters I couldn't go see it.

MARION: Well, I'm going to brave it. (*She exits*)

NILES: Careful! There's a peculiar, spiny-looking plant that I'm certain was not there when we parked the car.

ZAP: That's gonna do it. I been down here three days, it hasn't bothered me; now I can't go out.

NILES: So what is the news?

ZAP: They're saying soon now. Hi. (*This is to* DOHERTY *as he enters*)

DOHERTY: Yes, yes, yes—

NILES: Sorry for that absurd—

DOHERTY: No, no, no. The mission has seen everything. During the land-grant riots one of my colleagues was in his church when bullets came flying through the window. I'm afraid he packed his bag and left the keys to the church at the post office. I so much enjoyed your tirade. I love a good tirade, they're such fun. Talkers and tiraders. (*Singsong*) "I love a tirade."

NILES: I'm afraid I do tend to fly off the handle.

VITA: Like an ax blade.

DOHERTY: I was struck by what you said. Teachers with concern are rare. People don't always care by your age.

NILES: Thank you.

DOHERTY: Yes, it's unusual, I believe. Oh, you mean age— well, you can't do anything about that.

NILES: Thank you.

DOHERTY: No, by your age too many teachers have become cynical. Teachers and preachers. Dr. Don saw a lot of that, didn't you, Dr. Don? All that elbowing and getting ahead? Of course, he was at the top of his class; always dizzying to look down from those heights.

NILES: Are you? Congratulations.

DON: Thank you.

DOHERTY: Yes, one of the chosen. Many are called but only two are chosen. Dr. Indian Don and a bright young woman intern, Dr. Alice, who is not in my parish, being a Baptist. Not under my wing.

DON: I'm not under your wing, Father.

DOHERTY: No, you're making your way away.

DON: The first chance I get.

DOHERTY: Yes, he has to be in Santa Fe tonight. He's meeting the Great Man and the young woman intern, and the three of them are winging away to San Francisco. (*Sings lightly*) "Open your Golden Gate . . ." You are naturally proud to be one of the chosen two.

NILES: I'd think he would be.

DOHERTY: Pride indeed. Lambs, led to the slaughter. All very worrying. Vanity, vanity.

NILES: But why not? Vanity is only human.

DOHERTY: Yes, but then, what isn't? Aren't we very human, though? Sometimes I'm amazed at how very human everyone is.

DON: It has nothing to do with you.

DOHERTY: He's always telling me that. That's an impolite way of saying nobody asked you. And believe me, nobody did. I volunteered. (DON *storms out*) I think the wonderful thing about people is that if you leave them alone they'll do what their heart knows is right. If you only leave them alone. Long enough.

DON: (*Entering*) Where are the keys to my bike?

DOHERTY: Aren't they in your bike?

DON: You know where they are. Let me have them.

DOHERTY: Do I know where your keys are? He's always

trying to trap me into telling a deliberate lie. No, I don't know where your bike keys are. Exactly.

DON: I'm not going to do what you think I should.

DOHERTY: I have every confidence you're going to do what you think you should.

MARION: (*Entering, a small memo pad in her hand*) I got through; I have it.

ZAP: Oh, no.

DOHERTY: I've always felt—

ZAP: Excuse us, Father— Oh, boy. When do I play?

DOHERTY: Oh, you got through.

VITA: San Diego does exist.

MARION: Eleven in the morning.

ZAP: Oh, great.

MARION: I have the whole schedule. Your leg up to the final eight.

ZAP: (*Long pause*) You better read it to me. What does that look mean? It's good? Same old . . . ? You better read it.

MARION: Eleven in the morning, first match is Evans.

ZAP: Clyde Evans? (*Nod. A long pause—five seconds. Matter-of-factly*) That's no sweat.

MARION: Then the winner of the Baley and Syse match. Then the winner of Bouton and Tryne or Carey and Luff. Luff is seeded eighth, believe it or not.

ZAP: (*Beat*) Let me see. (*She hands him her note*) "Zappala–Evans, Baley–Syse, Bouton–Tryne, Carey–Luff." I can take Evans in straight sets—6–1, 6–1 if he lucks out. Baley–Syse is like a matching from the tadpole pool. Tryne gets mad, Carey is a fairy, and Luff—with all due respect to my fellow players, Luff is a cream puff. Evans, Baley, Syse, Bouton, Tryne, Carey, Luff. Woooo! Son-of-a— Woooo! I mean, I don't want to disparage true professionals who will, I'm sure, play up to their ability and with great heart, but this is a list of the seven most candy-ass tennis players I've ever seen. This is the Skeeter League. If I couldn't make the final eight in a— Where's Rose? Where's Charley Tick is the question. They got all those guys together on the other leg? What kind of a lopsided draw— Tryne does not possess a serve. None. Carey is, in all humility, probably the worst professional sportsman I've ever seen. What Paul Carey most needs is vocational guidance. Syse I have personally beaten four times without him winning one game. 6–zip, 6–zip. Zap! You candy-asses. Wooo! I gotta walk, I gotta walk. You charter the plane? (*Exits*)

MARION: He's waiting on the runway.

NILES: Is it really that easy a field?

MARION: Luff could be a problem, but I don't think so. It's so much luckier than any draw he's had—nothing's sure, but it's very fair. (*Enormous yell offstage. Everybody gets up, looks out*) No, it's just Zappy. He's okay. What do you know. What do you know. Son-of-a-gun.

NILES: That's remarkable. That's— (*Mumbles*) wonderful. Something like that.

VITA: What, love? Are you okay?

NILES: That's wonderful, I said. Dizzy, nothing. (*Sitting*) Did he leave his radio? Do we have a report?

VITA: Soon.

ZAP: (*Re-enters, furious*) Is that what they think of me? This is my class? What I should do is say forget it. If that's all the respect you got—if I ain't better than this—what this is is a public embarrassment. They're lucky if I show after this.

MARION: It's the luck of the draw. It's names out of the hat.

ZAP: That's not luck, that is a massacre. Okay. Okay. What I gotta do here is not get overconfident. What I gotta prevent is getting the big head. My paramount problem here is going to be not falling asleep, which, when you're facing Charley Baley across the net, is not an easy thing to do. Evans, Baley, Syse, Bouton, Tryne, Carey, Luff. Puffballs. Puffballs. Massacre. I gotta walk. I gotta walk.

DON: Zap, do you have the keys to my bike?

ZAP: Hell, no.

DON: You don't?

ZAP: But I don't mind lying to you like a priest would. (DON

makes a move toward him. ZAP *dodges*) I don't have 'em;
if I had 'em, I'd take a spin. Watch out, "Brave with Arrow,"
I'm fleet of foot.

DON: Forget it. (*He stands glaring at the wall*)

ZAP: I gotta walk, I gotta walk. (*He exits*)

DOHERTY: It's always possible that you lost them. You tend
to lose things lately. (*Beat*) Now, he's going to be stoic. I
used to think Ernie was calling him Elijah. I thought he
saw in Don the prophet of the Lord, fed by ravens, slayer
of the false prophets of Baal. It turned out he was calling
him Kow-liga. Kow-liga was a wooden cigar-store Indian in
some hillbilly song. (*Sings*) "Poor old Kow-liga." I don't
know why you think any of us would be opposed to your
success. Could you see a motive for anything but rejoicing,
Professor?

NILES: (*To* DON) He really does do that, you're right. (*To*
DOHERTY) I'm sure it's no one's business but his.

DOHERTY: My point exactly.

DON: Oh, sure.

DOHERTY: He doesn't trust a word I say.

NILES: I don't see the point in badgering the boy. It's his
decision.

DOHERTY: I'll have bad dreams about his silent indictment.
Imagine knocking cancer research. I'm sure they need every
man, woman, and Indian.

VITA: He might be the one who finds the answer.

DON: I think we will.

DOHERTY: We have great respect for your chosen field.

DON: When did you find out?

DOHERTY: Your great Dr. Noah Lindermann called me for a reference. I think he wanted to be reassured that you wouldn't scalp your co-workers. I gave you a glowing recommendation. I was surprised to discover you'd visited there. You neglected to mention it. Wined and dined, no doubt.

DON: Enough.

DOHERTY: It sounds like quite a place, Marion. Warm climate. Highest-paid researchers in the country. He didn't neglect to mention that. Most of the researchers, the Great Man told me, prefer to live away a bit. Houses along the coast road. Pleasant drive to work. Sunset highway.

MARION: Sounds like Los Alamos. Highest standard of living in the state.

DOHERTY: If you judge by creature comforts, as everyone does nowadays.

MARION: Everyone in the state resents Los Alamos, but the milk resents the cream.

DOHERTY: Your Great Man said he'd been impressed with the way you presented yourself. Thought you'd be useful eventually in an administrative position.

DON: He didn't say that.

DOHERTY: He did. Said you had agreed.

DON: I said I'd do what was necessary.

DOHERTY: I can see you now, making a grant proposal: belligerent and sincere. I told him you cleaned up nicely.

DON: The place is better endowed than any other in the country.

DOHERTY: Yes. They're better at it. Drafting a woman and an Indian. It's a wonder he didn't grab a black and a Chinese. Oh, they're probably already there.

DON: You don't know anything about it, Father.

DOHERTY: About what? Grantsmanship? I know nothing about that? I think this may be the first time in history someone in the Catholic Church has been accused of not knowing how to make money.

MARION: I think they'll love you. I see a turquoise belt buckle and maybe one earring.

NILES: Why not?

DOHERTY: Why not, indeed? It sounds like a wonderful life. Clean surroundings, intellectual problems, no patients, no pain, no filth, no ugliness. Only success. Even the rabbits and the mice are white.

NILES: It remains his decision.

DOHERTY: I have every confidence he will make the right choice.

NILES: You can't tell them what to do. No profit in it.

DOHERTY: Profit is the last thing I'm looking for.

NILES: (*He holds his hand to his head*) It isn't up to us to judge what's right—

DOHERTY: Judgment! Oh, my goodness. I quote chapter and verse on judgment. We are here, you and I, to show the light—teachers and preachers—

NILES: No, no. Who are we to say go one way or go another?

VITA: Don't get upset again.

DON: It's nothing to you.

VITA: Do you have a headache? You've had a little too much sun, maybe.

NILES: No, the—too much sun, I'd imagine. Just a passing fuzziness, it occurred a moment ago, outside. It passes. Don't look so alarmed. You're determined something should be the matter—what is the situation with our being held hostage here?

VITA: Soon.

MARION: Soon.

NILES: "Soon" means nothing. Soon is now. I see no reason why we couldn't pack the car. You hadn't intended to leave all this here, had you?

VITA: I thought perhaps not. We can put this in the car if you like.

NILES: I am sorry, I am irritable and I am antsy and quite cross and half-crazy, and I don't know at all why. But I do not intend to stay here any longer. Darling, do pick that up. (*She looks at him*) You open your hand, put your hand on the handle. You close your— I'll do it. Take that. I'll do it. Excuse us, it's been real as the—and my hat. (*As she just looks at him*) Leave it. Leave it. Get to the car.

MARION: You can't go anywhere until they lift the road-block.

NILES: You think they'll gun us down at the checkpoint? I think not.

MARION: It wouldn't be out of character.

NILES: If they don't let us pass, then we will either run the damn roadblock or wait there until they do let us pass. One can apply logic with amazing results if one tries. (VITA *is taking the keys from his hand*) What do you want?

VITA: I'll drive, you navigate.

NILES: I'll drive, thank you. Very— (*Mumbled word— supports himself against the wall*)

VITA: Something is not quite right with you, my dear, and you're not going to—

(NILES *slides to a seated position on the bench*)

DON: Has he eaten?

VITA: Very little; he hasn't been hungry, he said.

DON: Does he have diabetes? Does he—

VITA: No. I don't think so. He doesn't go to doctors— What, darling?

NILES: I thought I had passed out— Did I . . . ?

DON: Straight out on the bench—

VITA: (*As they stretch him out*) What's wrong?

ZAP: (*Running in*) Boy, he has really spooked me. I can't go out—

MARION: Sit, doll. Not now.

DOHERTY: It's all right. Don knows what he's doing.

VITA: So tell me.

ZAP: He passed out? Maybe you should put his feet up.

MARION: Cool it, Zappy.

DON: Is he usually as nervous as he's been here?

VITA: Only the last month; the last week or so it's been worse. Every other day or so.

DON: The perspiring is normal?

VITA: Not usual at all. I assumed it was the heat.

DON: It isn't that warm.

VITA: You're talking to someone from Rhode Island.

DON: I've never had the pleasure. Does he drink?

VITA: No, almost never.

DON: Has he had a drink today?

VITA: He doesn't drink. No. Sorry.

DON: What drug is he taking?

VITA: Only Valium. There were three. I squirreled the rest away.

DON: (*Presses* NILES'*s leg*) You feel that? (*The other leg*) That? Can you move it? (NILES *does*) This one? Arm? (NILES *moves one arm*) This one? (NILES *waves his hand*) Well, what the hell, we'll try the sugar. (*To* MARION, *pointing to the sugar and lemonade*) Put a lot of that in a glass of that stuff. (*Back to* VITA) You're sure he doesn't have diabetes? At least it can't hurt.

VITA: What is it?

DON: Who knows.

VITA: What's his pulse?

DON: Exceeding the speed limit a few miles. (MARION *hands him a glass of lemonade*, DON *and* VITA *help* NILES *to a sitting position*) Can you drink that?

NILES: Oh, Lord, no.

DON: Drink. It won't hurt you. (*To* DOHERTY) You should keep a medical cabinet here. I've told you that before.

DOHERTY: If you have to take him to Los Alamos, you can use my car.

VITA: Why would . . . ?

MARION: That's the closest hospital. It's at least two hours to Gallup.

NILES: I pray Gallup is a town and not a mode of transportation.

VITA: Do be quiet.

DON: Drink that.

NILES: I don't know why, but— (*Mumbles*)

VITA: Don't talk.

NILES: I said, I have every confidence in you. I can't imagine why.

DON: That's all, now. Close your eyes if you want. (*To* MARION) Do another. It's nothing. He's just faint.

ZAP: Oh, Jesus. (*Turns to go*) I can't go out there, the ants will get me.

MARION: Sit.

VITA: He's out cold.

DON: No, no. (NILES *opens his eyes*) Hello again. You don't have to open your eyes. Drink that. All.

What's wrong?

to MARION *for another lemonade, checks pulse*)

It could be any of about ten things. All this flying off the handle is not his typical behavior?

VITA: Not at all, no.

DON: And not eating. (*Though they talk, their concern is still with* NILES)

VITA: No, he's always been very predictable in his routine; very careful about his health.

DOHERTY: Until he made his dramatic denouncement to his class?

VITA: Yes.

DOHERTY: That must have been a surprise to you.

VITA: No, we went through his work together. I didn't completely agree at first, but I certainly saw his point. Actually, by the time he left the college, we were pretty much in agreement that it was the only thing he could do.

DOHERTY: All very brave. We always admire all that. And what are your plans after Singer's?

VITA: I don't know if we have any—

DON: (*Checking pulse*) I think that's slowing down to a trot now. That's amazing. Feel that. What do you know?

VITA: It seems weak.

DON: No, it's good.

NILES: If this has anything to do with radiation poisoning, I'll sue Chin Rock's ass.

DON: Who knows. Could be the heat if you're not used to it. Could be some kind of slight stroke, I don't think so. Stress, nerves, some sort of mild hypoglycemic attack. Could be . . .

NILES: I flatly refuse to suffer from hypoglycemia.

DON: Pulse doesn't speed up like that and then come back that dramatically in many instances.

NILES: No, no, it's much too "the thing to have." I couldn't possibly.

DON: Everyone likes to say they have hypoglycemia; it's no fun if you do. No way to be sure without an examination and tests. They have the facilities to fix you up at Singer's.

NILES: (*To* VITA) Could you bear my telling people—say at cocktail parties—that I'm feeling a touch palpitant from my hypoglycemic condition?

VITA: Grounds for divorce.

NILES: That's what I thought.

VITA: You're very tall to keel over in that way. You might 'urt someone.

'poglycemia. Is like you feel sweaty, and you get
    you don't have any energy?

        vou, I'm not joking.

ZAP: No, I'm cool. You're looking good, Professor.

NILES: I feel an utter imbecile. (*To* VITA) I seem to be coming apart at the seams on you, don't I? Everything is coming unglued all at once.

VITA: Not quite.

NILES: Not quite all at once, or not quite everything?

VITA: Not quite unglued.

DON: Sit. You're not going anywhere. Finish that.

NILES: Vile.

DON: Have one more.

NILES: Oh, surely not.

DON: No argument. They're small.

NILES: Anyone care to join me? I hate drinking alone.

DOHERTY: I think I will, actually.

MARION: (*With the thermos*) Would you like a little something in it?

DOHERTY: No, no. Not one of my vices.

MARION: You don't mind if I . . . ?

DOHERTY: Not at all. Any number of precedents.

MARION: Vita?

VITA: No.

DON: Go ahead.

VITA: I think maybe I will.

NILES: (*To* DON) That's amazing stuff.

DON: If we had a fifty-percent glucose solution, that reaction would have been instantaneous.

NILES: I refuse to believe all my histrionics can be ascribed to low blood sugar.

DON: It's . . . it's more complicated than that.

NILES: Things always are.

DON: (*Has scribbled on a notepad*) Give this to Admissions at Singer's.

NILES: (*Reading*) You really must be a doctor. This is completely illegible. There's a certain poetic justice. One would expect denizens of an "ivory tower" to have thin blood.

DON: Forget I said that. I wasn't thinking.

NILES: No, I thank you. I was walking around out there remembering. Though my student years were in earlier and what we like to think of as easier times—centuries ago, it seems—I remember having the same romantic impression of my professors' lives. Heaven knows, I'd never have gone into such a business otherwise. An edifice not at all unlike an ivory tower was my ignorant and egotistical hope those centuries ago. I actually envisioned a life of quiet reflection, strolling through the groves—the lot of it. We would go, a gentle band of enlightened teachers with quiet good humor, exchanging ideas with those younger minds entrusted to us, in a lively, perhaps even elegant symposium, with, we hoped, something like grace.

DOHERTY: But lately you experienced a—what did you call it? I liked that so much. You experienced a disturbance in your willful suspension of disbelief. Wonderfully articulate, those poets. It took me fifteen minutes to figure out what that could possibly mean. All those negatives. Disbelief. What a thing to require. But disbelief is rampant nowadays. People are running about disbelieving all over the place. But a willful suspension of disbelief is believing, isn't it? So a disturbance in one's willful suspension of disbelief is right in my wheelhouse.

NILES: Oh, dear.

DON: Comes with the territory.

NILES: When I started teaching I was a renegade, believed nothing, investigated everything. And subtly over thirty years I became absolutely dogmatic. This is true, that is false. *A* is better than *B*. *B* is superior to *C*. Look for *A* about you. Anyone today not able to accomplish *A* is no kind of artist at all. All very neat and formulated. And they copy it in their workbooks slavishly. *A* is better than *B*. Look for examples of *A*. They don't even realize they're being brainwashed. They don't care. The thing they most often ask is, "Is this going to be on the test?" Once, in a thousand students, someone says, "How do you know that?" "Why, good Lord, man, when you've looked at the art of the Renaissance for as long as I have, with utterly blind eyes, you'll know that too."

DOHERTY: So you blew the whistle on yourself; took yourself right out of the game.

NILES: The sporting move when I discovered I was useless.

DOHERTY: Then, like a silly, you stopped eating and made yourself sick. You threw it all away and looked up and saw yourself standing at a crossroads, and you looked down the wrong road at the wrong future and you saw nothing, of course, there's nothing down that road. But you can't do nothing, man. You have a young wife, the possibility of a family, I would think. What manner of person ought we to be? I'm afraid I'm not going to be able to refrain from preaching a little sermon tonight. The only good thing that can come from these silly emergencies, these rehearsals for the end of the world, is that it makes us get our act together. (*He takes the Bible from the altar*)

NILES: I'm in no state to follow you to the end of the world just now.

DOHERTY: Fortunately, you have a remarkable sense of self-preservation. (*Looking through the Bible*) Imagine storming out in such a beautiful rage and not saying: "And I quit." I wouldn't have been able to resist it.

NILES: I have that to look forward to.

DOHERTY: But you could go back next term as though nothing had happened.

NILES: I cannot go back. My only sure conviction is that teaching is harmful.

DOHERTY: I'm sure anyone as clever as you could find a way to teach that.

NILES: And how would that appear in the college catalog? Beginning Heresy?

VITA: Professor Harris on Heresy.

DOHERTY: Of course. What else? Heresy 101. But imagine the subterfuge necessary. You'll be like St. Peter meeting the early Christians in the catacombs outside Rome.

NILES: "Now, my children, this is the truth. Tell no one where you heard it lest we all be hanged for attempting to bring the whole bogus boondoggle down to its knees."

DOHERTY: Seven times around the wall, and on the seventh day they blew the trumpets and the walls fell down flat. My, my. I should have been a rabbi. I love those old Hebrew tales. Subversives were always being hidden by harlots in every well.

NILES: If there was a way to survey my subject without comment, without comparisons. "This is a painting. What does it say to you? There will be no test, make friends where you like." Oh, dear. Given today's students, begging for structure, half the class would have breakdowns within a week.

DOHERTY: (*With a Bible*) Ah ha!

VITA: What?

DOHERTY: This is the end of the world. (*Reading*) "The day of the Lord will come as a thief in the night; in the which the heavens shall pass away with a great noise, and the elements shall melt with fervent heat. The earth also and the works that are therein shall be burned up. Seeing then that all these things shall be dissolved, what manner of persons ought ye to be in all holy conversation and godliness?" It seems appropriate tonight to remind ourselves of that. And you are a teacher. So you simply have to find a way to teach. One of those professions, I've always thought, one is called to. As an artist is called, or as a priest is called, or as a doctor is called.

ZAP: That "call," man, that's the moment, man. That's magic. That's magic, that's magic.

MARION: What, doll?

ZAP: No, that magic that happens and you know who you are, you know? Like, "I'm a doctor, is what I do." Or, "I teach kids." Or like Marion.

MARION: Hardly.

ZAP: No, no joke. She said—you told me—I want to show artists' work. Like Van Gogh's brother. He was—

MARION: Theo.

ZAP: Yeah. Or like when I found out I was a tennis player.

VITA: I love you.

ZAP: No, no joke. I went to church and lit a candle, man.

DOHERTY: You give thanks for that light.

ZAP: Really. I said my novenas, man, 'cause it had been like a—not a miracle that anyone would know except just me— but it had been like when those girls saw Our Lady of Fatima up on that hill. It was really weird. I was like in the fifth grade and I was watching these two hamburgers on some practice court, and they took a break and one of them hands me his racket. So I threw up a toss like I'd seen them do and zap! Three inches over the net, two inches inside the line. There wasn't nobody over there, but that was an ace, man. You should have heard those guys razz me. I mean, you know, they say, "Man, you stink." And all those things you can't repeat in front of a priest. They was really on my case. And I think that's the first time anybody ever looked at me. I mean, I was skinny, you've never seen—most of the girls in my homeroom had about twenty pounds on me. So this guy shows me a backhand grip and he hits one to me and zap! You mother! Backhand! Right down the line. And the thing is, that's where I wanted it. I saw the ball come at me, and I said I'm gonna backhand this sucker right down the line, and I did.

So then they took their ball back. Which I don't blame them, 'cause no high school hotshot is gonna get off on being showed up by this eleven-year-old creep that's built like a parking meter, you know?

But that was it. I hit that first ball and I said, "This is me. This is what I do. What I do is tennis." And once you know, then there's no way out. You've been showed something. Even if it's just tennis, you can't turn around and say you wasn't showed that.

So I went to church and said a novena for those meatballs 'cause they didn't know all the butterflies that was in my stomach, that they'd been my angels. But, man, on the way home, anybody had asked me what I did, right there I'd have said, "I play tennis." Didn't know love from lob, didn't matter. That's what I am. 'Cause once you know what you are, the rest is just work. (*Pause.* DON *nudges him with his foot*) Whatta you kicking me?

DON: Get up.

ZAP: It ain't like I got a lot to do, you know? There's not even a paved area and a wall to hit a ball against.

DON: Get up off the bare floor. That's the worst thing you could do to yourself. (*Beat*) Half the aborigines in the world have arthritis by the time they're twenty from lying on the bare ground.

ZAP: Don't start with diseases, okay?

DON: Are you relaxed? Your muscles are loose? You're hanging out? You feel loose?

ZAP: Are you kidding? I'm cold, I'm stiff; I'm about as loose as a fireplug.

DON: Lie on a bench, don't lie on the bare floor.

ZAP: Now, see, I'll remember that. I retain things.

(*The helicopters return. Over their sound microphones blare:* THE ROAD IS CLEAR. THE ROAD IS CLEAR)

DOHERTY: Isn't that wonderful. Playing with their toys.

HELICOPTER: *The road is clear!*

DOHERTY: Listen to them. (*To the door*) You've given us all our monthly dose of fear, now fly back to White Sands and gloat. Shame. Shame! Don't they love to scare us to death. Don't we love them to do it. Can't you feel the tingling? Isn't fear exciting?

VITA: I could do without it.

DOHERTY: Well, maybe you can. Most people are beginning

to look forward to these little emergencies. These shows of power. They've always wanted a big terrible God of the Old Testament and now they have Him. They want to see the fiery cloud. Don't tell me they don't.

(*The helicopters are making another sweep.* DOHERTY *goes out the door. They are directly above him*)

HELICOPTER: *The road is now clear!*

DOHERTY: The road is not clear! You're sick as cats! You've made the bomb your god and you're praying for the bomb to call in the number. Well, you'll get it if you don't watch out. The Archangel Gabriel will announce the second coming of the Son of Man, and this time his voice will be a siren. (*The helicopters go off*) Oh, I get so angry with everyone. Look at how foolish I am. (*He comes back in, brushing dust off his shirt*)

NILES: You shouldn't have been a rabbi. You should have been a foot-washing Baptist.

DOHERTY: They do, they worship energy. Dear, dear. We've regressed to the caveman, astonished by fire. Compare a diddly bomb on this diddly planet with the divine design of the universe. Some silly astronomer said to me on a radio program that the universe started with a Big Bang, and I said: "Yes, you know that, and I know who pushed the button."

MARION: You've taken to speaking on the radio?

DOHERTY: No, local talk panels about goodness knows what. The program's been running for twenty years; by now they're scraping the bottom of the barrel. My superiors aren't happy about it. They'd like to send me somewhere. But there's no place left to send me.

VITA: And you wouldn't go.

DOHERTY: Oh, wild horses. No, someone has to stay. If every rational person leaves, the vultures will pick the Indian clean. The Spanish and the Anglos have good hospitals, so what do they care if the Indian has shockingly inadequate medical facilities. With Don leaving, they'll have almost no help at all.

DON: Come on.

DOHERTY: We had hoped for an improvement after all these years.

NILES: I believe I see a drift back to your thesis. You don't let up.

DON: I was expecting it.

DOHERTY: As well you should have. The professor could tell you. You left the college because you thought you'd been bought. I'm sure you recognize the purchase of someone else.

NILES: You really are shameless. All those stories of his childhood, dragging a stethoscope around—

DON: That's one of his favorites.

DOHERTY: You sit there and don't overtax yourself. You know nothing of the situation here. The Indians have one hospital for the Navaho, the Zuni, the Hopi . . .

DON: The Jemez, the Zia, the Laguna, the Acoma, the Apache . . .

DOHERTY: The Indian doesn't go to the hospital until he's nearly beyond hope. Until this Noah Lindermann Don had been planning to travel from pueblo to pueblo.

NILES: Much as you do.

DOHERTY: Much as I do. "Seeing that all this world shall be dissolved, what manner of persons ought we to be?" That man is a doctor. He has been a doctor since he was five years old. The man has been called. If you think I'm going to let the devil take him away from his people—

NILES: Hardly the devil—

DOHERTY: Oh, many fancy disguises, and don't forget it. I've never talked to anyone so smooth, even on the telephone, in my life.

NILES: I'm sure you set great store by him, but what he wants to do with his life is no concern—

DOHERTY: The need here is something you can't comprehend.

NILES: Need be damned. Need is not the question.

DOHERTY: (*To* DON) Weren't you called to be a physician? Didn't you kneel here at this altar with me and pray after you told me you had been called to help your people?

DON: I was eleven years old.

DOHERTY: Have you been called now to alter your course?

DON: Shut up, Father.

DOHERTY: Have you, have you? Did you hear a voice saying to you: "Leave your people and leave your land and go with this great television personality"? Did you?

DON: I discovered I have a very special talent for research; if that's hearing a call, then I've been called.

DOHERTY: No, you just decided you can't turn down this opportunity for a better personal life. Maria knows it, your uncle is shouting it to the sky right now, and you know it too. You know what manner of person you ought to be.

DON: You are tearing me apart!

NILES: (*To* DOHERTY) You don't care a damn what he does for *him*.

VITA: What do you care?

DOHERTY: Your brightest star jumped in the bay. What would you have done if you had the chance? This is my brightest star. Ten seconds from now he'll be in midair over the water. What would you do?

NILES: You cannot hold power over another man; even for his own good. This is your foster child. You see your reflection in him. I've seen it with teachers a dozen times. I've done it myself.

VITA: Not now.

NILES: You want that for you. You may be right as rain, but you're doing it for yourself. I don't know if that's Christian, but it's certainly not kosher.

DON: Don't talk.

DOHERTY: No. Don't say anything for a moment. I'm think-ing. (*Pause. He goes to the window and looks out for a long while. When he turns around, there are tears in his eyes*) I don't know that it matters, but you're right. I was thinking of myself. Well, well . . . vanity, vanity. You seem to be almost fit, Professor. Don, you're to be congratulated. Now, I'm holding Mass not too long from now, and there are things I have to do. (*He picks up the tray with pitcher and glasses*) Will you need this again?

DON: No, Father.

NILES: I may have been a bit severe for a disinterested stranger.

DOHERTY: No, no. I'm very thickheaded. Only approach, only approach. Very thickheaded me. But I'm right, young man, and you know it.

DON: I knew you'd think so.

DOHERTY: Right as rain you said—we don't get much of that here. You think we should let them make up their minds; I'm not above blackmail and bludgeoning.

NILES: We can only present the case. I imagine you've shown a rather remarkable example.

DOHERTY: No, no, too common. Working with the common people, as they call them in their ignorance, is very common. (*To* MARION) Well. Those asinine helicopters said the road is clear. They were more truthful when they said the bridge is out. (*He carries the tray into the residence*)

VITA: (*To* ZAP) You have a plane to catch.

ZAP: Yeah, the cars are moving. Oh, boy, now I don't want to go.

MARION: Sure, sure you do. Get our stuff; don't run off without the radio.

NILES: You feel they should check us all into a hospital to monitor the radon count in our blood. Not that they could do anything about it.

MARION: I'll settle for leaving.

ZAP: I'll drive; I'm too drunk to sing. Keep my mind busy.

MARION: (*As* DOHERTY *returns*) So. Listen. We have to go. I'll see you.

DOHERTY: No, no . . . actually you won't.

MARION: Thanks, Father Doherty. You were a good friend . . . to . . . all of us.

DOHERTY: I take more than I give.

MARION: Don't we all? Vita.

VITA: Marion, good luck. Good meeting you.

MARION: Under any other circumstances.

NILES: I'm pleased about your draw.

ZAP: I can't think about it. Oh, uh—Father. Do you think you could bless me? I mean not so I should win, I wouldn't want to take advantage of the other players, but just so I shouldn't fall over my feet, you know, and make Marion look like a fool.

DOHERTY: Sure, sure. One of my specialties. (ZAP *kneels.* DOHERTY *mumbles*) May almighty God bless you in the name of the Father, of the Son, and of the Holy Spirit.

MARION: Take care of yourself.

NILES: I intend to. You as well.

DOHERTY: Don't forget to give Don the keys to his bike.

ZAP: Oh. He said hide 'em, don't tell me where you put them. I gave them to Marion. Come on. 'Bye, now. Vita; Professor.

VITA: 'Bye now. Nice meeting you, Zappy.

ZAP: Doctor.

DON: Zap. Ace 'em.

ZAP: Right on. (*Exits*)

MARION: I almost forgot. (*She takes the keys from her purse, tosses them to* DON. *He catches them, looks at her for a moment. She goes*)

VITA: How far is the airport?

DOHERTY: Only an hour and a half. He'll get a good night's sleep.

(*There is a car horn*)

VITA: That's Zappy. I love him. He reminds me of my brother.

(*They all move to the doorway, looking out. The horn fades away, honking repeatedly*)

DOHERTY: I cheated. I said, "Make him win." (*Pause*) Look who's pumping water over there.

VITA: Is that the old woman who won't eat?

DOHERTY: Mrs. Valdez. I think she's changed her mind. I made a pact with her granddaughter. The little girl pretended to be deathly ill, and the old lady had to get up to take care of her. Deathly ill, deathly ill. I'm very good at applying Band-Aids, but sometimes the parishioners are only suffering from scratches.

(*They turn away from the doorway*)

VITA: It's so beautiful here.

DOHERTY: You be careful. Most of the residents came just to look and never left.

VITA: I wouldn't mind that.

NILES: I can imagine us living here as well as I can imagine us living anywhere.

DOHERTY: You can't think right now. Who could? You're exhausted. Look at you.

NILES: Thank you. Everyone keeps telling me.

DOHERTY: You need a good rest and you're going to get it. Then you're going to sneak back to work and you're going to raise Cain. That's not exactly the way a priest should put it, but . . .

NILES: Like Peter outside the gates of Rome. Peter was crucified upside down, as I remember.

DOHERTY: But in a good cause. Which reminds me, I've invited your wife to stay for Mass. It must have been years.

NILES: That's thoughtful of you, but—

DOHERTY: She accepted.

VITA: It was my idea.

VITA: I think I've forgotten the responses.

DOHERTY: They come back. It's like riding a bicycle, you don't forget. I speak Navaho, and they reply in Navaho. A little broken Latin will work in beautifully. (*Exits into the residence*)

NILES: (*To* VITA) Would you like to stretch your legs? Then we can come back.

VITA: I'd like that.

(DOHERTY *returns. Puts the Mass kit on the altar steps*)

NILES: (*To* DON) It won't hurt to walk a little?

DON: It won't do you any good. You should sit and rest.

NILES: Just a short turn. To the road and back.

DON: Why did you ask?

284745

Hill

NILES: Thank you, by the way, Doctor. If I haven't said that.

DOHERTY: That's what he's here for.

NILES: Or there for.

(DOHERTY *spreads the two cloths on the table that serves as an altar.* VITA *and* NILES *look at* DON *a moment, then exit into the garden.* DOHERTY *sets out two little vials—wine and holy oil, then two candlesticks and two candles*)

DON: (*After a long pause*) I'm glad I saw you.

DOHERTY: (*Sets out two goblets, and covers one*) Me, too. Don By-the-River.

DON: Tabaha.

DOHERTY: (*Sets up cross*) No, no, By-the-River. Don By-the-River. Like the song. (*Sings lightly*) "Don-by-the-riverside." Dr. Don. I've been too fond, young man. Too fond.

DON: Me, too, Father.

DOHERTY: Yes, yes . . . well . . . (*He goes to the altar, lighting the two candles*)

DON *is crying. He looks around the church, picks up his duffel bag, and leaves.*

DOHERTY *turns from the altar and moves to the window. The motorcycle starts up. The sound fades away.* DOHERTY *turns back, looking to the altar. After a moment he checks his watch and walks slowly outside and begins ringing the bell to call the congregation to Mass as the lights fade.*